ALED JONES'
FAVOURITE CHRISTMAS CAROLS

Also by Aled Jones

Aled Jones' Forty Favourite Hymns

ALED JONES' FAVOURITE CHRISTMAS CAROLS

Aled Jones

preface
publishing

Published by Preface Publishing 2010

10 9 8 7 6 5 4 3 2 1

First published in Great Britain in 2010 by Preface Publishing

20 Vauxhall Bridge Road
London SW1V 2SA

An imprint of The Random House Group Limited

www.rbooks.co.uk

Addresses for companies within The Random House Group Limited
can be found at www.randomhouse.co.uk

The Random House Group Limited Reg. No. 954009

A CIP catalogue record for this book is available from the British Library

ISBN 978 1 84809 120 7

Penguin Random House is committed to a sustainable future for
our business, our readers and our planet. This book is made from
Forest Stewardship Council® certified paper.

Printed and bound in Great Britain by Clays Ltd, Elcograf S.p.A.

Design by Peter Ward
Typeset by Palimpsest Book Production Limited,
Falkirk, Stirlingshire

To Claire, Emilia and Lucas – my love

CONTENTS

INTRODUCTION

I suppose if you asked people which particular season they'd associate me with it would be Christmas, probably because I recorded 'Walking in the Air'. I don't have a problem with that because Christmas is my favourite season and this is to do with carols. This seasonal music is fantastic. It uplifts the soul, it makes you feel happy whether you're listening to it belted out on a system in some park, or sitting outside a department store in America, or in a supermarket in a British town. Hearing these songs of Christmas that are all about the birth of Jesus makes you feel glad to be alive.

I've sung carols for as long as I can remember and love doing it. There's spellbinding power in this music. I've vivid memories of school assemblies and concerts where they were sung with great gusto and maybe out of tune; even back then performing them made me feel good. As a small boy I had the opportunity of a lifetime when I sang 'O Holy Night' at the exact spot where Jesus was born in Bethlehem. I was also lucky enough to join Bangor Cathedral as a chorister and we felt special conveying the Christmas message to our congregation through song – people felt festive and they were elated by these magical pieces.

One of the things that has surprised me in writing this book is the really rich variety of types of carol that have been collected by the great carol hunters like Percy Dearmer or Ralph Vaughan Williams. I've tried to reflect some of this variety, selecting some folk carols, lullabies and cradle songs, songs of slavery, Latin antiphons, even a counting game. These carols also span the centuries. The earliest was written round about the ninth century, the latest are modern and recent. I also wanted to have both classics that have stood the test of time and been top carols in the *Songs of Praise* polls and a good number of lesser-known gems.

Quite a few of the carols in this book have a childlike quality about them, which in my view makes them particularly special. That some of the melodies are uncomplicated and easily learned is a good thing. How magnificent that a carol like 'Away in a Manger' is simple enough for a child to sing and understand. Equally wonderful is that 'Away in a Manger' is also a terrific carol to perform as an adult. When I was a child I loved this carol's idea of asking Jesus to be forever at my side and I love that idea to this day. As far as I'm concerned, Christmas would not be Christmas without these musical gifts.

Although not all the carols in this book are my favourites, all of them are here because they have special merit of some sort that is worth putting to you, whether it be well-written words, a wonderful melody, or the fact that they've really connected with human beings. I think it will be obvious which are my favourites, and they will probably be among those of a great many people.

What I like and value are simple, heartfelt melodies, which have words that can touch the soul and bring out the best in us. There's something otherworldly about 'Silent Night', 'Jesus Christ the Apple Tree', 'Away in a Manger', 'In the Bleak Midwinter', for example. They almost have healing qualities, they make you feel better when you're singing them. And it doesn't have to be that you're performing them in a church, or a hall, or a cathedral setting, they can even be sung in the shower. There's something very particular about singing Christmas carols.

I've been given the chance to go out to Israel on a number of occasions and to sing Christmas carols in some of the most religious places in the world. This has had a profound effect on me – it's brought carols to life in a larger and deeper way. I also went to Flanders filming for my ITV programme at the spot where British and German troops would have sung 'Silent Night' at dead of night, with hatred and fear and anger in the air. How could I begin to imagine what it was like for those soldiers to hear that lovely melody being sung? It must have produced in them sadness and longing, and brought back memories of loved ones at home. Once I experienced that feeling out there in Flanders, this carol took on

a completely different meaning for me. Before then I'd sung it knowing that it had a fine melody and a good story around it; now it has a gritty reality to it. I've had many such experiences, performing these carols in places where they've changed people's worlds and its been an honour to delve deeper into the lives of some of them for you.

Away in a manger

W.J. Kirkpatrick

A - way in a_ man - ger, no_ crib for a bed, The_

lit - tle Lord Je - sus laid_ down His sweet head. The

stars in the_ bright sky looked_ down where He lay, The_

lit - tle Lord Je - sus a - sleep on the hay.

1

AWAY IN A MANGER

WORDS
Unknown, 1885 (verses 1 & 2),
verse 3 attributed to Charles H Gabriel (1856–1932)
or John Thomas McFarland, (1851–1913)

MUSIC
'The Cradle Song' by William J Kirkpatrick (1838–1921),
'St Kilda' by J E Clark (no dates)
'Mueller' by James Ramsey Murray (1841–1905)

I

Away in a manger, no crib for a bed,
The little Lord Jesus laid down his sweet head.
The stars in the bright sky looked down where he lay,
The little Lord Jesus, asleep in the hay.

The cattle are lowing, the Baby awakes.
But little Lord Jesus, no crying He makes.
I love thee, Lord Jesus, look down from the sky.
And stay by my side until morning is nigh.

Be near me, Lord Jesus, I ask thee to stay
Close by me forever, and love me, I pray!
Bless all the dear children in thy tender care
And fit us for heaven, to live with thee there.

This is an intense carol with a strong message put across in a way everyone can understand, yet its life-story reads like a whodunnit. Who wrote the words? Who wrote the tune? The origins of 'Away in a Manger' are, as with many other carols, shrouded in doubt.

These days it is accepted that the author of the first two quiet stanzas is unknown. Bishop William F Anderson remembered that while he was Secretary of the Board of Education in England between 1904 and 1908, Dr John T McFarland, then Secretary of the Board of Sunday Schools, dashed off a third stanza. However, earlier in 1892 the book *Gabriel's Vineyard Songs* by Charles H Gabriel includes the selfsame third stanza. So Bishop Anderson's story loses credibility: the alibi is blown!

For decades, the credit for both the words and the music went to Martin Luther who was supposed to have written them for his five-year-old son, Hans. Nothing has ever been found among Luther's works to confirm this. But a clue in his favour is that Luther did write and compose some marvellous hymns, for example 'Out of the Depths I Cry to Thee' of 1523 and 'A Safe Stronghold Our God is Still' (1529). Still, it's generally thought these days that this is a wrong deduction and that the lyrics are based on a poem written for the 400th anniversary of Luther's birth in 1883. Another proposition is that the theory that Luther is the 'culprit' may have been dreamed up for an early and, it seems, effective, marketing ploy: Luther as writer lent the song greater authority than would the anonymous credit 'North American origin'. North America was still a young country and rather short on history. Whatever the truth, Martin Luther has become the red herring in this mystery. Now it looks as if he had nothing to do with either the words or the music.

So, if not Luther, who wrote the music? In December 1945, Richard S Hill, a musical historian, holed himself up in a dusty library and, turning detective, isolated as many as forty-one musical settings for the carol. He investigated further and came up with four likely suspects. These men were mentioned in more collections than the others and were backed by the most evidence. They were James R Murray, 1887, John

Bunyan Herbert, 1891, Charles H Gabriel, 1892 and last but certainly not least, William J Kirkpatrick, 1895.

Once a carpenter (fitting for the man who wrote this heart-warming carol involving a carpenter and his wife), William J Kirkpatrick devoted himself entirely to music after his first wife died in 1878. Fifteen years later, according to a snippet in the *New York Times* in 1893, Kirkpatrick married Sara K Bourne at noon on 23 October that year. We know for sure that in 1895 William wrote a simple piece called 'Cradle Song'. In the UK 'Cradle Song' is usually sung to the words of 'Away in a Manger', its unpretentious tune reminding us of music's power to move.

But with other versions there is less certainty about who composed what. In 1895, the *Little children's book: for schools and families. By authority of the general council of the Evangelical Lutheran Church in North America* was published and 'Away in a Manger' is present, listed as a nursery hymn. Here, and in many publications following, the tune is called 'St Kilda' and the author is J E Clark of whom I can find no further trace. Two years later, on 7 May 1887, James R Murray (1841–1905) compiled *Dainty songs for little lads and lasses, for use in the kindergarten, school and home.* Murray made the apparent mistake of saying the tune is 'by Martin Luther for his children' and of putting his initials where the composer is usually credited. This led to the idea that he had arranged a work by Martin Luther who it was supposed wrote the music and the words. Over the next two years Murray tried to correct this. He published a new edition with his own music transposed into G major with the all-important credits: 'music by JRM'. In the next edition he put his initials only and reverted to his original score.

Murray would have been familiar with the thorny jungle of copyright law and have known that an arrangement of an old song is protected. Many compilers of song collections in the nineteenth and early twentieth centuries assumed old compositions to be in the public domain and would include an arrangement rather than ferret out the original, so infringing the arranger's copyright. Murray committed an own goal by attributing his own arrangement to Martin Luther. After this, many carol

anthologies included his arrangement, carrying on the myth he had helped to create.

Then in 1921 a collection was published that would trailblaze the idea that a Carl Mueller wrote the music to 'Away in a Manger'. Little is known of Mueller, and Richard C Hill has suggested that an editor, suspecting that the German priest and theologian Martin Luther was not the composer, made up a name as a plausible substitute for the actual creator or arranger of the piece. To add to this confusion of identity, the equally gentle melody 'Mueller' by, in fact, Murray, was sung to the carol which was first known as 'Luther's Cradle Hymn'. It is this version of 'Away in a Manger' that is most often sung in North America.

As we have seen, in the UK, there is no doubt about who composed 'Cradle Song', the tune traditionally sung to the words for 'Away in a Manger'. It is the American composer William J Kirkpatrick. This version of 'Away in a Manger' was voted fifth out of a top ten of carols in a 2008 UK poll carried out to mark the launch of a Barbie DVD! More than seventy-five per cent of respondents said that singing carols made them feel nostalgic; they associated carols with childhood when Christmas is the most exciting time of the year, so it's not surprising that they chose this as one of their top ten.

On the night of 20 September 1921, William Kirkpatrick, aged eighty-three, apparently told his wife Lizzie (by now he had married for the third time) that he had a tune in his head and would not come to bed until he had written it down. When Lizzie Kirkpatrick awoke later, her husband was not there. She found William at his desk. He was dead. Perhaps this was a fitting close to a long and productive career: after his death Kirkpatrick's wife assigned the rights for 1,049 of his hymns to a publishing company, only a portion of his total output. Whatever the tune William Kirkpatrick heard the night he died, the melody he wrote fifty years before is simply sublime. It's a perfect demonstration that simplicity doesn't have to be boring.

I first came in contact with 'Away in a Manger' at Llandegfan primary school. I remember a feeling of great warmth flooding over me

instantly. Singing the song felt really good. It has been one of my favourite carols since that special moment in school assembly all those years ago. I sing it often these days – as often as I can, and I've done so all my career, boy and man, in cathedral settings, concert halls and even in far-flung destinations like Israel.

It's interesting to note that many professional choirs shy away from programming this carol as part of their Christmas concerts and services because it's seen as childlike in its construction. I think they're missing a trick on this one. It's that very childlike quality that means it's a song that connects instantly and paints a vivid picture of the Nativity. When singing it you almost feel like you're there, part of the scene. There seems to be a warm glow around the whole telling of the event.

My favourite verse is the third, which is probably the most childlike: it's a simple prayer for God to be present in all of us from childhood innocence throughout our lives, until we all meet again in Heaven:

> Be near me, Lord Jesus, I ask thee to stay
> Close by me forever, and love me, I pray!
> Bless all the dear children in thy tender care
> And fit us for heaven, to live with thee there.

This carol is a gem. It's one that has had a huge impact on my life and I'm sure will continue to do so.

2

CALYPSO CAROL

'See Him Lying on a Bed of Straw'

WORDS AND MUSIC
Michael Perry (1942–96)

COPYRIGHT
Mrs B Perry/Jubilate Hymns

6

See him lying on a bed of straw:
A draughty stable with an open door;
Mary cradling the babe she bore:
The Prince of glory is his name.

Oh now carry me to Bethlehem
To see the Lord of love again;
Just as poor as was the stable then,
The Prince of glory when he came.

Star of silver, sweep across the skies,
Show where Jesus in the manger lies.
Shepherds swiftly from your stupor rise
To see the Saviour of the world.

Refrain

Angels, sing again the song you sang,
Bring God's glory to the heart of man:
Sing that Bethlehem's little baby can
Be salvation to the soul.

Refrain

Mine are riches from your poverty,
From your innocence, eternity;
Mine, forgiveness by your death for me,
Child of sorrow for my joy.

Refrain

The 'Calypso Carol', or 'See Him Lying on a Bed of Straw' is a modern song, although it is now nearly fifty years since it was composed. The calypso rhythm has led some to assume that this carol comes from the West Indies and perhaps this was underlined when in 1983 the Caribbean island of Nevis issued the song's refrain on a set of postage stamps. In fact Michael Perry, the writer of this carol, was born in Beckenham, Kent in 1942 and wrote this piece aged twenty-two while still at college. His inspiration was a Christmas question put to some young people: 'How would you like to be born in a stable?' Well, 'Calypso Carol' responds, on a bed made of straw in a 'draughty stable with an open door'.

Canon Perry went on to become one of the UK's leading contemporary hymn writers, and this one became his best-known composition through a very mid-twentieth-century mishap. When the tape of a carol service for BBC radio was accidentally wiped, Cliff Richard came to the rescue and recorded an alternative. One of his choices for the recording was 'See Him Lying on a Bed of Straw' and a hit was made.

The lyrics speak of the wealth that Christ has brought to the world and remind us of the significance of his birth. Through the innocent baby's poor beginnings in a 'draughty stable' and his later crucifixion, our flaws and transgressions can be recognised and forgiven. It is important, the song tells us, to remember that Jesus paid a price for our wellbeing. The third out of a total of four verses outlines how our riches – our way of life, not material wealth – are only possible because of Christ's sacrifice: 'Mine, forgiveness by your death for me/Child of sorrow for my joy.'

This carol asks us to reflect on God's message. It is perhaps all too easy to forget that peace or happiness are hard won: others have made sacrifices to make it possible. In the third verse 'Calypso Carol', like many traditional carols, evokes the Angels who witness our daily lives. It asks them to remind us and 'Sing that Bethlehem's little baby can/Be salvation to the soul.'

Michael Perry was a major figure in the religious music world. He was a founding member of Jubilate, an organisation set up in the sixties to offer an alternative kind of song to younger worshippers who were influenced by popular music. Perry was part of a movement to create songs that stepped outside the traditional musical and lyrical expectation of hymns. Such songs are called 'contemporary worship music', or 'praise songs' and have become very much a part of services held in many Anglican churches today. 'Calypso Carol' is an early example of this music.

Besides his work in the church and his busy musical career, Canon Michael Perry did much towards clarifying copyright issues for writers and composers of worship music. He countered the objections of critics who considered that songs written in praise of the Lord should not provide economic benefit to their authors. Jubilate, with which Perry was involved for the whole of his career until his death from a brain tumour in 1996, now represents over seventy authors and composers including David Iliff, co-editor of *The Carol Book*. Since 1966 Jubilate has been a major publisher of praise songs and prayers for many of which Michael Perry was the editor. In 1969 Jubilate published *Youth Praise 2*, one of the leading collections of contemporary worship music. It included Perry's 'Calypso Carol'.

There are varying suggestions as to the roots of the musical style of calypso. However, it is likely the style is of African origin: in the eighteen hundreds, slaves working on plantations were not allowed to

talk but they were allowed to sing. The calypso was a way of protesting, of telling stories and communicating news around Trinidad and the other Caribbean islands. The subversive nature of the music alarmed the authorities, who in 1884 banned the playing of skin drums. The calypsonians, undeterred, adopted bamboo as their instrument. When this too was outlawed they resorted to found objects like pans and pots, which they fashioned into instruments. The 1930s saw these develop into the steel bands of today. The steel pan is the national instrument of Trinidad and Tobago and the only acoustic (non-electric) instrument invented in the twentieth century.

So, far removed from the traditional hymn, the calypso might be thought a bold genre for Michael Perry to choose for his carol, which has a typical calypso rhythm. However, he was tapping into the craze for calypso around the world and particularly in the US at that time. This had begun when, in 1956, Harry Belafonte released *Calypso*, an album that included the calypso 'Banana Boat Song', 'Day-O'. This was the first gramophone long-player ever to sell a million copies; it topped the charts for thirty-one weeks that year.

'Calypso Carol' was introduced to me through *Songs of Praise*. I'm sure I must have heard it at some point when I was a child, though we didn't really sing it at school. But it's definitely one I remembered pretty instantly when I heard it on *Songs of Praise*; it's a first-rate example of the result of marrying a good melody with good lyrics. With its upbeat rhythm it raises the spirits and encourages an energy that reflects the excitement of those following the star on that particular night. It has found the right blend of the secular and the religious and has touched our hearts. 'Calypso Carol' was voted one of the UK's top ten favourites in the *Songs of Praise* poll of 2005.

It's a great melody to sing, with a very catchy refrain that needs everyone to give extra volume, especially on the line: 'The Prince of glory when he came'. I don't think it will be one that I'll try to record on my own. I think it definitely needs a choir or a big congregation to deliver it at its best. I love singing it as part of a traditional congregation on

CALYPSO
CAROL

9

Songs of Praise because the members of the congregation never know how to move or dance or tap their toes or tap their sides – its always a rather uncomfortable moment. Although if you've got a fantastic gospel choir singing it as well, it makes the process a lot easier.

3

COVENTRY CAROL

WORDS AND MUSIC
Anon.

Lully, lulla, thow littel tyne child,
By, by, lully, lulla.
Lullay, lulla, thou littel tyne child,
By, by, lully, lulla.

O sisters too, how may we do
For to preserve this day
This pore yongling
For whom we do sing
Bye, bye, lully, lulla?

Herod, the king,
In his raging,
Chargid he hath this day
His men of might
In his owne sight,
All yonge children to slay.

That wo is me,
Pore child, for thee,
And ever morne and say
For thi parting
Neither say nor singe:
'By, by, lully, lulla.

Lully, lullay, thou little tiny child,
Bye, bye, lully, lullay.
Lully, lullay, thou little tiny child,
Bye, bye, lully, lullay.

Oh sisters too, how may we do
For to preserve this day.
This poor youngling
For whom we do sing,
Bye, bye, lully, lullay?

Herod the king,
In his raging,
Charged he hath this day
His men of might
In his own sight,
All children young to slay.

That woe is me,
Poor child, for thee,
And ever mourn and sigh
For thy parting
Neither say nor sing:
'By, by, lully, lullay.'

Haunting and sad, the 'Coventry Carol' has deep roots and an unusual history. It's said that the melody and lyrics originated in the songs that Bethlehem women sang when they held their firstborn sons during King Herod's reign of terror. It's rare in the history of carols that the ordinary people caught up in the Christmas story speak directly to us. Here it is the mothers themselves who sing this dark and frightened lullaby to their babies: 'Lully, lulla, thow little tyne child'.

The carol was first performed formally in the sixteenth century in Coventry as part of a mystery play called *The Pageant of the Shearmen and Taylors*. The play would proceed through the streets of the town, with the players performing on carts and the audience followed on foot – it must have been quite a sight. It brings to vivid life the Christmas story in chapter two of Matthew's Gospel, which has at its centre the Slaughter of the Innocents.

Herod, the king of Judea, is visited by the wise men who prophesy the wonders of Christ's birth. Wily Herod, who wants to find and kill the baby, says to them: 'Go and search diligently for the young child; and when ye have found him, bring me word again, that I may come and worship him also.' But the wise men, having found the child and presented him with their gifts, are warned in a dream not to return to Herod, and go home another way. Matthew continues in these stark words: 'Herod, when he saw that he was mocked of the wise men, was exceeding wroth, and sent forth, and slew all the children that were in Bethlehem, in all the coasts thereof, from two years old and under.'

The 'Coventry Carol' was performed in the play at the point where the women are singing to put their children to sleep lest Herod's soldiers find them by their crying. A splendid stage direction notes, 'Here Erode ragis (Herod rages) in the pagond (pageant) and in the strete also.' Its music is plaintive, full of the fear of impending brutality, but also the loss felt by the mothers. The play goes on to show what happens next, when the soldiers arrive to murder the children – one of the women stands up to them, flourishing 'the womanly geyre' of her 'pott-ladull'. But

her resistance is futile. Then, as Matthew puts it, 'was there a voice heard, lamentation, and weeping, and great mourning'. Written for three voices, the carol would actually have been sung by a boy, and two men, representing the women, which audiences would have been used to.

The Coventry cycle was first mentioned in 1392 but the tune of the 'Coventry Carol' was first recorded in print in 1591 and the lyrics in 1534. Many of the traditional carols we sing today have lost their original tune or lyrics, but this one has kept both. Their author or authors however are unknown and a fire destroyed the manuscript at the Birmingham Free Reference Library in 1879. So in one sense the lyrics we sing today are original, but they are based on poor-quality transcripts and may not be completely accurate. The music has been recovered from a manuscript engraving also considered inaccurate – Thomas Sharp's *Dissertations on the Pageants or Dramatic Mysteries, Anciently Performed at Coventry . . .* (1825). It is a well-known example of a 'Picardy third' (a harmonic device used in European classical music) and is traditionally sung a cappella.

There is much discussion about the meaning of the words – for example, 'And ever morne and say/For thi parting/Neither say nor singe' in the last verse isn't clear. Some writers have changed it to 'ever mourn and may' some to 'ever morn and day'. Other writers have given the meaning as plain 'grieve and sigh'. I sing simply, 'And ever mourn and sigh/For thy parting/Neither say nor sing.' Like other medieval carols, the 'Coventry Carol' is lesser known than the big hits like 'We Three Kings of Orient Are' or 'Hark! The Herald Angels Sing' (both nineteenth-century). Today it is mostly sung not by congregations in church services but by choirs in Christmas performances – a far cry from the colourful outdoor pageants of sixteenth-century Coventry.

I first got to hear 'Lully, Lullay' at Bangor Cathedral when I was a probationer looking up at the main choristers. It was during one of the Christmas services that I heard this carol which sounded so different to all the others that we sang. It's neither bright and energetic nor similar in vein to something like 'O Come, O Come, Emmanuel!' The melody is like that of no other carol, including the fact that the final chord goes into the major when the whole of the music has been very much in the minor. It's odd to think that as children we used to sing this carol whose lyrics are quite heavy going, being all about the danger that these babies could be in. But the story makes it really, really powerful to sing as an adult. Even now when I perform it I approach it in such a different way to all the others, it's almost as if you need to take greater care with 'Lully, Lullay' because it's so haunting and emotional that it requires more concentration and more from the heart. You've got to delve deep into your soul to bring out the best in this carol.

It's almost impossible to imagine what any of these mothers felt like, or fathers for that matter, under the threat that your child would not just be taken away from you, but would be murdered. The melody line up until the final chord is quite ploddy, it doesn't really do anything out of the ordinary. But then you get this huge shock on the final phrase when you expect the melody to go da da da da da with the final da the same note as the preceding, and it goes da da da da da and the final da goes up with a major leap – something that you're really not expecting. Maybe it's there because on the final chord there's some hope that murder won't be the downfall of your newborn baby and that God will come good in the end – who knows? The carol was performed at a highly dramatic moment near the end of *The Pageant of the Shearmen and Taylors.* I can imagine the lights going down in the performance space and basic-ally just the words and the music telling the story. It doesn't need any gimmicks at all.

Due to a lot of repetition in the words, the 'Coventry Carol' harks back to some of our greatest hymns, which use repetition to great effect. This doesn't happen so often in carols, but in this one it does. It's very still, it's thought-provoking in its construction; it makes you listen.

4

THE ANGEL GABRIEL FROM HEAVEN CAME

(Gabriel's Message)

WORDS
Basque carol collected by
Charles Bordes (1863–1909)

MUSIC
'Gabriel's Message' arranged by
Edgar Pettman (1866–1943)

Translation by Sabine Baring-Gould (1834–1924)

The angel Gabriel from Heaven came,
His wings as drifted snow, his eyes as flame:
'All hail,' said he, 'thou lowly maiden Mary
Most highly favoured lady.' Gloria!

'For know a blessed mother thou shalt be,
All generations laud and honour thee,
Thy Son shall be Emmanuel, by seers foretold.
Most highly favoured lady.' Gloria!

Then gentle Mary meekly bowed her head,
'To me be as it pleaseth God,' she said.
'My soul shall laud and magnify his holy name.'
Most highly favoured lady. Gloria!

Of her, Emmanuel, the Christ, was born
In Bethlehem, all on a Christmas morn,

The angel Gabriel

(Gabriel's Message)

adapted by
S. Baring-Gould

Traditional Basque

The an-gel Ga-bri-el from hea-ven came,___ His

wings as drift-ed snow, his eyes___ as flame.___ 'All

hail' said he, 'thou low-ly maid-en Ma ——— ry,___ Most

high-ly fa-voured La — dy, Glo ——— ri-a!'

And Christian folk throughout the world will ever say:
'*Most highly favoured lady.*' *Gloria!*

This beautiful, melodic Basque carol brings to life the Annunciation and Mary's lines in St Luke's Gospel: 'Behold the handmaid of the Lord, be it unto me according to Thy word'. The moment when the Angel Gabriel comes to Mary and tells her she will be carrying the son of God must have been like a thunderclap to this 'lowly maiden' Mary. Luke says simply, 'and the angel came unto her'. The carol tells it in splendidly dramatic – and suitably scary – form: 'The Angel Gabriel from Heaven came/His wings as drifted snow, his eyes as flame'. The Angel Gabriel calls Mary 'most highly favoured lady'. The feast of the Annunciation on 25 March was known, and still is in many parts of rural Britain, as Lady Day.

Sabine Baring-Gould wrote standing up. The author of memorable hymns like 'Now the Day is Over' (often heard chiming from belfries) translated 'The Angel Gabriel' from the original Basque carol. Renowned for ten-minute sermons, with which his congregation seemed comfortable, Baring-Gould wrote another of his hits, 'Onward Christian Soldiers', within a similarly short time frame while a teacher at Lancing College near Brighton. He was a multi-talented man. Besides his clerical duties and attending to his brood of fifteen children, he was a novelist and scholar. With so much to do no wonder he had little time to sit down!

Baring-Gould's background was far from calm or uneventful. One of his ancestors, Edward Gould, murdered a man who had beaten him at the gambling table. Edward got off on a technicality familiar to readers of murder mysteries: his counsel proved that a witness could not have identified him by the light of the 'full moon' as the moon had not been full that night. Edward's gambling might have cost him the family seat of Lewtrenchard Manor had he not already mortgaged it to his mother Margaret, known as Old Madame. Margaret Gould disapproved of the religious beliefs of her daughter's husband, Charles Baring (of the banking family) and insisted that he add 'Gould' to his name and that the estate go to her grandson, Sabine's grandfather.

Sabine's father, also Edward, worked for the East India Company. His career was curtailed by a carriage accident and then Edward took the young Sabine abroad. This meant he spent little more than two years in formal schooling. One winter spent in the Basque country may have been the inspiration for his translation into English of this old Christmas carol which he called 'The Angel Gabriel from Heaven Came' or more simply, 'Gabriel's Message'. Unable to transcribe a tune, Baring-Gould sang it to himself until he could remember it and then got a member of his family to note it down.

Baring-Gould's desire to take holy orders was disapproved of by his father, but despite threats of disinheritance in 1864 he became curate at Horbury Bridge in the West Riding and he did take over the estate on Edward's death in 1872. Then in 1881, when his uncle died, he became both parson and squire (squarson) of Lewtrenchard Manor for the last four decades of his life. The manor today is a hotel, complete with the desk at which Sabine wrote 'Onward Christian Soldiers' and with rumours of the ghost of Old Madame; the house is supposedly little changed since Sabine's painstaking renovations.

Sabine's grandson William Baring-Gould was an expert on Sir Arthur Conan-Doyle's Sherlock Holmes. He wrote a biography of this famous, but fictional, detective, *Sherlock Holmes of Baker Street: A life of the world's first consulting detective*, which was published in 1962. Short of material for Holmes' early years, William is supposed to have drawn on the eccentric experiences of his grandfather Sabine for inspiration. An early case of identity theft!

The Basque carol, '*Birjina gaztetto bat zegoen*', which Baring-Gould translated, was included in the *Archives de la Tradition Basque* collected by the French music teacher and composer Charles Bordes and published in 1895. Co-founder of the Schola Cantorum, Bordes was part of a successful movement to open up the French music scene in the nineteenth

century from its focus on opera to music that included plainsong. The Schola Cantorum is now a highly respected institution with alumni such as the cellist Paul Tortelier and composer Cole Porter.

Aside from Bordes' source it's been suggested that the roots of this carol go back to a fourteenth-century Latin chant, 'Angelus Ad Virginem'. There are also several versions of 'The Angel Gabriel', including one by the Victorian poet Gerard Manley Hopkins (1844–1889) called 'Gabriel From Heaven's King' and another by an unknown author, 'The Angel Gabriel from God', which is published in the 1833 edition of *Christmas Carols Ancient and Modern*.

In this and other of his translations, Baring-Gould does not provide a literal English version of the text; instead he captures the essential atmosphere of the original. He reduced the number of stanzas from six in the original to four, and used powerful imagery, writing in fine phrases reminiscent of the Victorian era in which most of his life was lived. Sung with few instruments or with a choir only, not only for the Annunciation, but for Advent and Christmas services of lessons and carols, this is a moving meditation on the magnitude of God's choice of Mary to be the mother of his son and on her humble response to the message that Gabriel brings to her. The words were first published in *The University Carol Book* in 1922 of which the composer Edgar Pettman (1866–1943) was music editor.

Sabine Baring-Gould died a week after Christmas Day, on 2 January 1924. He is buried next to his wife Grace, the mill girl he had fallen in love with when she was 16, in the churchyard across the road from Lewtrenchard Manor. It is to be hoped that after 90 years of a full and productive life, which includes this wonderful carol, this energetic, gifted man rests there in peace.

I think I was first introduced to 'The Angel Gabriel' by the musical supervisor of *Songs of Praise* and I included it on my first Christmas album as an adult, sung to an oboe accompaniment. My favourite verse is the third, which is the only time we hear Mary speak:

Then gentle Mary meekly bowed her head,
'To me be as it pleaseth God,' she said.
'My soul shall laud and magnify His holy name.'

The writing is old-fashioned, but it's still relevant to this day. It's another carol that, without having an obvious melody, is musically both exciting and interesting. My favourite part to sing is definitely the final 'Gloria!' because it's very lilting, very melodic and you can put a lot of different emotions into each of the 'Glorias' at the end of each verse. It's a favourite with choirboys around Christmas because the Lady becomes flavoured as opposed to favoured – and the Lady of course is called Gloria!

Performing this piece of music was definitely one of the highlights of my Christmas tour a few years back during the time I was also doing *Strictly Come Dancing*. This carol just does seem to lilt along and it's a real pleasure singing it. I feel I put my whole soul into it. It's also one of those carols that could never become stale. I performed it forty-seven times over fifty-two nights on that tour and every night found something different within those four verses.

The clever writing of this carol means that musically it grows throughout the verses – the first growing into the second, second into the third and third into the fourth. The words do exactly the same thing, so that every verse has a starting point and then a climax and then you start again and then a climax, start again and to a climax . . . This is carol writing at its best; I like it so much that I gave my son the middle name of Gabriel.

5

DECK THE HALL WITH BOUGHS OF HOLLY

'Nos Galan'

WORDS AND MUSIC
Anon.

Deck the hall with boughs of holly,
'Tis the season to be jolly,
Don we now our gay apparel,
Troll the ancient Yuletide carol.

See the blazing Yule before us,
Strike the harp and join the chorus,
Follow me in merry measure,
While I tell of Yuletide treasure.

Fast away the old year passes,
Hail the new, ye lads and lasses,
Sing we joyous all together,
Heedless of the wind and weather.

Carols are of course associated with Christmas and the birth of Christ. This is not how they started out. At the beginning, carols were pagan and they were sung (and danced) for festivities and rites that had nothing to do with Christmas or Christianity. The medieval church adopted carols to celebrate the major feasts and 'Deck the Hall' is a fine example of carols' long journey of reinvention from pagan festival dance songs through to current Christmas carols.

Until researching this book, I'd not known that the tune for 'Deck the Hall' was Welsh. But it was originally a Welsh dance song dating back to the sixteenth century and sung at Yuletide accompanied by the harp. Yuletide is one of those pagan religious festivals that have been absorbed, like carols, into the Christian church, as in the case of Yule into the celebration of Christmas. Yuletide was originally observed from late December to early January and was placed on 25 December when the Julian, Christian calendar was adopted.

'Deck the Hall' goes right back to the beginning in another way. One of the various interpretations of the origin of the word 'carol' is that it means a dance – a circling dance. 'Deck the Hall' began as just that, a circling dance. On New Year's Eve, revellers would dance in a ring around the harpist, who played answering bars to the verses improvised or remembered by the dancers. It was like a party game – if a dancer could not think of a new verse, he or she would drop out of the dance. It's thought that the 'fa la la la la, la la la la' refrains now sung in the carol replace the harp's responses. And the harp is here in the lyrics, with 'strike the harp and join the chorus'.

'Deck the Hall' celebrates the harp – an instrument understood and appreciated in Wales. The tune was first found in a musical manuscript by Welsh harpist John Parry Ddall (*c.*1710–1782; in Welsh, Ddall means blind, so his name was blind John Parry), but it is without a doubt older than that. It was published in 1784 by harpist Edward Jones, who was an energetic promoter of the traditional music of his native Wales. He gathered more than 200 songs and even supplied prizes for harp-playing at the eisteddfod. For this carol (at the time a dance song), Jones uses the name '*Nos Galan*' (New Year's Eve) and the text of a love song written by the Poet John Ceiriog Hughes (1832–87).

Hughes also celebrated the harp of Wales. He worked for much of his life on the railways, as station master for Caersws railway station. He was celebrated for the simple directness of his poetry; like many Welsh

poets, he took a bardic name – 'Ceiriog' – from the River Ceiriog, which flows through the Ceiriog Valley, where he was born. In his home village, the public library contains a memorial inscription to him. He also spent his time pursuing his interest in the folk music and songs of Wales and the harpists who accompanied them, setting these old tunes to his own lyrics. This led to a grand project to publish four volumes of Welsh airs, of which only the first volume actually made it to press in 1863: *Cant O Ganeuon* ('A Hundred Songs').

During the eighteenth century the tune of 'Nos Galan' spread widely, but the Welsh harp was abandoned when Mozart used the tune in a piano and violin duet and, later, Haydn arranged it in the song 'New Year's Night', accompanied by piano, violin and cello.

No one seems to know who wrote the words of 'Deck the Hall'. We do know that the song was carried to North America by Welsh miners who emigrated to the Appalachian mountains of North Carolina, so the words may have American roots. It's clear though that they almost certainly bear no resemblance to the original words sung in the Welsh pagan festival or to the poem by John Ceiriog Hughes. The dance steps of the merrymakers are also lost.

The journey of *'Nos Galan'* continues into Victorian England. The carol was reinvented again when the Victorians started to understand Christmas not as a community event, but as a domestic festival honouring the family, with holly, and gifts, and trees. The Victorians turned 'Deck the Hall' into a traditional English Christmas carol. The first English version appeared in *The Franklin Square Song Collection*, edited by J P McCaskey in 1881.

Due to the pagan roots of carols, for many years the Church was uneasy about singing them. 'Deck the Hall' still wears its pagan clothes well. 'Deck the hall with boughs of holly,' it goes, ''Tis the season to be jolly.' The birth of Christ is not here, but the passing of the old year and the birth of the new are, and both are welcomed joyfully by everyone. Decking the halls with holly is an ancient custom several thousand years old – the Druids, Romans and Greeks all decorated their homes with

this plant. The Druids in particular believed that the holly was a sacred tree – they noticed that it remained green all winter long and thus believed that it was never deserted by the sun. The Romans considered holly to be a symbol of good will and sent wreaths of it to newlyweds as a token of good wishes and congratulations. Holly was also used during the festival of Saturn, which was held each year beginning on 17 December to honour the Roman god of sowing and husbandry.

In the twenty-first century and in the spirit of its pagan origins, 'Deck the Hall' fell into the hands of vandals. *Bart Simpson's Guide to Life* features the following:

> *Decorate your father's belly*
> *Fa la la la la, la la la la*
> *While he's sleeping by the telly*
> *Fa la la la la, la la la la*

Through all its reinventions, 'Deck the Hall' has remained a popular carol – dancing optional. It wasn't one we performed particularly often in primary school and the only time I think I have sung it was as a member of the Bangor Cathedral choir, not in the cathedral setting but in the concert setting at Penrhyn Castle, where we used to give Christmas concerts. It's a little bit too schmaltzy, too jolly for me and I like my carols with a little bit of a story, a little bit of a journey, and let's face it, this one has none of that. But through all its reinventions 'Deck the Hall' has remained a popular carol and the tune has stood the test of time. But, like Bart Simpson, I don't take it one hundred per cent seriously. It's programmed into a concert in order to put a smile on the face and it's one of those moments where you reach across and hold your child's hand and squeeze it gently.

 **6**

DING DONG MERRILY ON HIGH

WORDS
George Ratcliffe Woodward
(1848–1934)

MUSIC
Jehan Tabourot
(1518–93)

25

Ding dong merrily on high,
In heaven the bells are ringing,
Ding dong, verily the sky
Is riv'n with angel-singing:

Gloria . . . Hosanna in excelsis!

E'en so here below, below
Let steeple bells be swungen
And 'Io, io, io!'
By priest and people sungen.

Gloria . . . Hosanna in excelsis!

Pray you, dutifully prime
Your matin chime, ye ringers!
May you beautifully rhyme
Your evetime song, ye singers.

Gloria . . . Hosanna in excelsis!

'Ding Dong Merrily on High' – or as every chorister calls it, 'Ding Dong' – is one of those Christmas carols that probably everyone has sung during their lifetime and it's a little bit of Christmas cheer in the middle of a doubtless highly focused nine lessons and carols service.

George Woodward, who arranged 'Ding Dong', just missed being a Christmas baby, being born on 27 December 1848 in Birkenhead. He was ordained deacon in the Church of England just before Christmas on 21 December, aged twenty-six. He played the euphonium and his hobbies were bee-keeping and bell-ringing. He must have brought his bell-ringing skills to the writing of 'Ding Dong Merrily on High', keeping the bells swinging with a rhythmic rise and fall. It's a rhythm that is vital for the tune of the carol to succeed and it is the tune here, with its momentum of bells, that creates the dynamism of this carol, sweeping up the singer in a tide of euphoria.

Like many carols, including 'Deck the Hall' and 'The Twelve Days of Christmas', 'Ding Dong Merrily on High', which was first published in *The Cambridge Carol Book* in 1924, has secular beginnings with no seasonal or religious associations. George Woodward dug deep into the history of traditional European folk tunes to source his several carol collections. In this case he found the melody, *'Le branle de l'official'*, in a dance manual called *Orchésographie*. Published in 1589, this lively book is presented in the form of a dialogue between a dance tutor and his pupil, a device used today to make dry or difficult information easier to grasp. The editor, Thoinot Arbeau, was a French ecclesiastic, who had a penchant for anagrams, Thoinot Arbeau being an anagram of his real name, Jehan Tabourot.

Arbeau's book covers a range of late Renaissance dances as well as the branle, including the gavotte, the pavane and the volta. Unusually for the time, the musical score is set down one side of the page with the dance steps printed next to the notes. The exhaustive and sometimes exhausting dancing instructions in the *Orchésographie*, alongside woodcut illustrations of dancers in a variety of eye-catching costumes, leave nothing

to doubt. The branle appears to be similar to the modern line-dance and each one has a colourful title such as the 'branle of the horse', or 'the torch', or 'the washerwoman'. This 'branle' is danced, writes Thoinot/ Jehan, 'by lackeys and serving wenches', comprising 'little springs' whereby the lackey helps the serving wench to leap into the air. Sometimes the gentility liked to dress down as peasants and shepherds and dance like them too. This was perhaps because with so many intimate moves and steps, it was a good way to meet a future partner!

Despite its sixteenth-century origins, 'Ding Dong Merrily on High' is a carol of an early twentieth-century Christmas. It came upon the scene in the 1924 edition of *The Cambridge Carol Book* where it was arranged by the Irish composer and lecturer Charles Wood (1866–1926) who collaborated with Woodward on many of his books.

During the second half of the nineteenth and the beginning of the twentieth century carols moved indoors: from wassailing in the streets, they were brought into the more formal setting of the church. So 'Ding Dong Merrily on High' is a fine example of the secular dance – an original meaning of the word carol – coming together with the religious to create the inspirational song for Christmas that we think of today as a carol.

Carols have developed over centuries in accordance with cultural or religious shifts, with changes in words and verses. 'Ding Dong Merrily on High' started life in a very different social setting to today's. The carol's flexibility is represented in the variety of artists who have recorded it in differing arrangements. These include John Rutter and the Choir of Clare College, Cambridge, Maddy Prior and Charlotte Church. Alison Moyet's strong and melodious performance in the 1988 French and Saunders Christmas Special is backed by a berobed choir (French and Saunders). Singing with a lusty lack of harmony, they grab their microphone stands and come to centre stage, their soaring voices drowning Moyet's solo.

So, dance and bells and perhaps bees may be influences behind Woodward's compilation of this carol that rings in the powerful mystery of God coming to earth in human form. It brims with the vigorous energy of its secular roots, its tune leading the way.

I first performed 'Ding Dong' not at school, funnily enough – it obviously wasn't very popular in North Wales – but in Bangor Cathedral, and for me, as any chorister would probably tell you, it's always about breath control. I've heard so many choirs singing this piece of music and I was probably guilty of this myself in the early days in Bangor Cathedral, where you'd start the Gloria not having taken enough breath and so when you've got to the end of it you've no breath left to actually finish off the phrase. So the 'Hosannah in Excelsis' would be just a mumble. You feel you've really achieved something quite momentous when you can actually do the Gloria all in one breath without turning green or looking as if you've just run a marathon. It's also all about diction – the words need to be really spat out. And there are plenty of opportunities to roll the rr's: 'rriven wth angel-singing' and 'verrrily the sky' and I remember as a boy soprano not quite understanding what was happening in the second verse when the steeple bells are swung and 'io io io'. I'd sing it with gusto but didn't really get the intricacies of the message of the carol. Even if you don't get it, the chorus particularly tells you what it's all about – glorification and lifting your voice to God in song.

I'm not sure if 'Ding Dong' would be on my top ten list, I think it's probably a little bit too light-hearted and simplistic for my liking. And I don't mean simplistic in the way of 'Away in a Manger'. That simplicity works in its favour whereas this is really just a cheery Christmas interlude. I think lots of choirs record 'Ding Dong Merrily on High' to prove, especially on a Christmas album, just how versatile they can be. There have been some very elaborate arrangements of this carol, where lots of voices sing against one another, and on the whole I think that, though most of the best-known arrangements work, some have been too clever for their own good and by complicating this carol you take away its heart and it's overriding message.

7

O COME, ALL YE FAITHFUL

(Adeste Fideles)

WORDS & MUSIC
John Francis Wade (1711–86)

Translated by Frederick Oakley (1802–80),
William Brooke (1848–1917)

O COME, ALL
YE FAITHFUL

29

O come, all ye faithful,
Joyful and triumphant,
O come ye, O come ye to Bethlehem;
Come and behold him,
Born the King of Angels;

O come, let us adore him!
O come, let us adore him!
O come, let us adore him, Christ the Lord!

God of God,
Light of Light,
Lo! He abhors not the Virgin's womb;
Very God,
Begotten, not created;

Refrain

O come, all ye faithful

ADESTE FIDELES
translated by F. Oakeley,
W.T. Brooke and others

J. F. Wade

See how the shepherds,
Summoned to his cradle,
Leaving their flocks, draw nigh to gaze!
We, too, will thither
Bend our hearts' oblations;

Refrain

Sing, choir of angels,
Sing in exultation;
Sing, all ye citizens of heaven above;
Glory to God
In the highest;

Refrain

Yea, Lord, we greet thee,
Born this happy morning;
Jesu, to thee be glory given;
Word of the Father,
Now in flesh appearing;

Refrain

It wouldn't be Christmas if we didn't wholeheartedly perform 'O Come, All Ye Faithful'. It's one of those carols that have come to mean Christmas. It issues a personal invitation to witness the momentous event of Christ's birth – 'O come ye, O come ye to Bethlehem/ Come and behold Him/Born the King of angels'. The clear imagery of 'O Come, All Ye Faithful', which tells the story of Christmas from the virgin birth to the arrival of the shepherds and the three Magi, seems to have appeal for everyone, everywhere. It ends with the actual greeting of the newborn Jesus and an offering of praise and adoration to Our Lord now manifest in the world. It is sung with conviction in church services on Christmas Eve or Christmas morning when a celebration is called for and we respond with joyful assent and full hearts.

So it is perhaps strange to discover that this accessible hymn has such obscure origins and that theories abound as to who wrote the lyrics and composed the tune. It has been suggested that the music of 'O Come All Ye Faithful' was adapted by Handel or written by a prominent eighteenth-century Catholic musician Thomas Arne (1720–78). For many years it was an anonymous Latin hymn, 'Adeste Fideles', possibly written and composed by John Francis Wade, who was the son of a Leeds cloth merchant. If he did write it he may have copied the tune from other sources including, curiously, a 1744 comic opera, Acajou, by Charles Favart. John Francis was a Catholic and supporter of the Jacobite cause for the return of the Stuarts to the throne of Britain and, round about 1745–46, during a Jacobite rebellion, he fled to Douai in France. There he perfected his mastery of calligraphy and illumination and scratched a living by making and selling beautiful copies of plainchant and other music, as well as by teaching Latin and church song. He has been credited as the 'father of the English plainchant revival'. It's supposed that he wrote 'Adeste Fideles' some time around 1740 to 1743. A mystery surrounding 'O Come, All Ye Faithful' is why it became known as the 'Portuguese hymn'. It was regularly sung at the chapel of the Portuguese Embassy in London, and it was suggested that it had Portuguese origins, being composed by King John IV of Portugal (1603–56), 'the Musician King'. Ian Bradley suggests that Marcos Portugal (1762–1830), composer of opera and Chapel Master to the Portuguese kings, wrote the music. Whatever its origins, it grew in popularity from the mid-nineteenth century boosted by its inclusion in the first edition of Hymns Ancient and Modern in 1861.

The current text seems to be the work of many hands. The first, second, sixth and seventh verses, the most commonly sung, are based on a translation by Frederick Oakley (1802–80) for his congregation at the Margaret

Chapel in London. Frederick Oakley was keen to restore what he regarded as authentic church worship. He wanted to counter 'frivolous' modern tunes replacing them with tunes from older traditions. Criticism of his ritualistic practices contributed to his decision to embrace Roman Catholicism in 1845. Among those who worshipped at his Chapel, the Margaret Chapel in Marylebone, was William Gladstone, who liked the fact that the worship was both devout and hearty, and approved of the fact that the sermons never lasted for more than twenty minutes.

Verses three, four and five are based on a translation by William Brooke (1848–1917), who became interested in hymnology after entering commercial life. He apparently translated three new Latin verses and inserted them into the Oakley translation, thus forming the basis of the version that was first published in *Murray's Hymnal* in 1852 and which we sing today.

The mystery deepens in the early twenty-first century; Professor Bennett Zon, Head of Music at Durham University, has suggested that this carol contains secret codes from Jacobite times, the work of John Francis Wade. He thinks it masks an ode to Bonnie Prince Charlie, so that the 'all ye faithful' are in reality the Jacobites and 'Bethlehem' is England. Looked at in this way, 'O Come, All Ye Faithful' is about the restoration to the British throne of the exiled King Charles Edward Stuart – the Bonnie Prince – who was born on 20 December 1720. So, Professor Zon argues, the carol's hidden text is 'O come, faithful Catholics, joyful and triumphant, O come ye, O come ye to England; come and behold him born the King of the English – Bonnie Prince Charlie!' The carol would have lost its Jacobite meanings as Catholics gained more religious freedom and the Jacobite cause lost its attraction in the late 1770s. This coincided with Wade's (alleged) first publication of this glorious carol and its steady rise in popularity in churches of many denominations since then.

I sang 'O Come, All Ye Faithful' at school, I sang it in Bangor Cathedral. It's a carol that you really need to be able to perform with other people, best sung as a congregational carol. I've also sung it as a solo and it doesn't really work as well, it's very difficult to get the energy across that's needed, but when you've got like-minded people letting rip with you, then I think the true meaning of this carol comes across. It's performed at its best in St George's Chapel just before Christmas as part of my charity The Story of Christmas when you put the band of the Irish Guards with the descant (descant is musical ornament – it's the melody sung above, and simultaneously with, the main theme) and you've got the Choir of Westminster Cathedral, and a congregation of about 800 people. The way we do it is to break it up so that basically the carol starts with the magnificent fanfare, with all eyes on the horns of the Irish Guards, then as the carol is performed, a procession with the Bishop of London at the back comes to the altar and after

> Sing, choir of angels,
> Sing in exultation,
> Sing, all ye citizens of heaven above;
> Glory to God
> In the highest;

and the chorus, all of a sudden the light is taken down and the Bishop of London addresses the congregation with the final Lesson. I'll always remember that the first time I did it I was in the company of such fine actors as Judy Dench and Anthony Hopkins and down came the Bishop of London, Richard Chartres, and boomed the final Lesson in his most actorly of voices. You could see every well-known actor turn and face him and all that was going through their minds, which was what was going through mine, the fact that the Bishop of London had a better acting voice than any of those assembled. So what happens is that he reads his Lesson and then the band, voices of the choir, organ, all of us carry on to end the carol with 'Yea Lord, we greet thee/Born this happy morning' and it's a really special moment where you can understand how music is vital to worship. You have the words of the Bishop, which are so important, surrounded by this glorious music composed with God in mind. It's the perfect coming together of words and music in the most perfect of environments.

Many descants have been written for this carol, but I think that the best by far is by David Willcocks. It was published in 1961 in the first book of the *Carols for Choirs* series that we used at Bangor Cathedral. It's majestic, exciting, vocally challenging, and fits beautifully with the original melody. Another testament to this beautiful carol is that it can be performed away from a church or a cathedral setting and still retain its religiousness. I've been very fortunate to sing it in the Royal Albert Hall on many occasions, not just during a *Songs of Praise* Christmas recording but as part of Christmas concerts there and this carol's magnitude makes even the Albert Hall seem like a religious venue.

Another of my memories of this carol is of travelling with my wife, who used to work for the travel industry, flying out to San Francisco before her because the flight she was on was full and actually sitting outside Macy's store in the square in San Francisco with Christmas music coming out of a microphone and the whole of San Francisco it seemed in a good mood and hearing Bing Crosby singing this song '*Adeste Fidelis*', 'O Come, All Ye Faithful'. It was a real moment when you knew that Christmas was coming and there was a reason to be joyful.

Aside from Bing, this carol has been covered by everyone: Andy Williams, John Williams, Sinatra, Dylan, the Three Tenors, the Chieftans, Celine Dion, Enya – the list is endless. But 'O Come All Ye Faithful' is not a carol that I can say I really love to sing. I can't put my finger on why this is, because it has all the ingredients of a fantastic carol: it's majestic, exciting to sing, it has a powerful accompaniment, the words are very positive. But I think that for this carol really to come alive you need more than that somehow; you do need the descant, the brass accompaniment, you do need the blaring organ, and more than anything you really do need a fine congregation.

8

DO YOU HEAR WHAT I HEAR?

WORDS   MUSIC

Noel Regney (1922–2002)   Gloria Shayne (1923–2008)

36

Said the night wind to the little lamb,
'Do you see what I see?
Way up in the sky, little lamb,
Do you see what I see?

'A star, a star
Dancing in the night
With a tail as big as a kite,
With a tail as big as a kite.'

Said the little lamb to the shepherd boy,
'Do you hear what I hear?
Ringing thru the sky, shepherd boy
Do you hear what I hear?

'A song, a song
High above the tree
With a voice as big as the sea,
With a voice as big as the sea.'

Said the shepherd boy to the mighty king,
'Do you know what I know?
In your palace warm, mighty king,
Do you know what I know?

'A Child, a Child
Shivers in the cold,
Let us bring Him silver and gold
Let us bring Him silver and gold.'

Said the king to the people ev'rywhere
'Listen to what I say!
Pray for peace, people ev'rywhere
Listen to what I say!

'The Child, the Child
Sleeping in the night
He will bring us goodness and light,
He will bring us goodness and light.'

At Christmas there are many kinds of music, performed in churches, school assembly halls, community centres: all the places where people come together to celebrate the season. We hear Christmas songs on television and in shopping malls and cafes as we go about our lives buying gifts for our family and friends. Traditionally these are the carols that we have known since childhood, but many are not the classic compositions, they are modern Christmas songs. One such is 'Do You Hear What I Hear?'

'Do You Hear What I Hear?' was to be the 'B' side for a single expected to be a hit. The composer Noel Regney wrote the words picturing a new-born lamb. His then wife, the composer and lyricist Gloria Shayne, composed the tune. It's a great story, the fact that it begins with a little lamb, as not many carols do, and the fact that it starts with a night wind telling the lamb, the lamb tells the shepherd boy, the shepherd boy then tells the mighty king and the king proclaims the story of this magical child that has come to save us all. The hook of the whole carol is one single line if you like. It's 'Do you see what I see, Do you hear what I hear, Do you know what I know, listen to what I say' – that's it in its entirety.

It's also a prayer for peace. In October 1962, at the time this song was written, the world was contemplating the very real possibility of nuclear war. Russia had placed nuclear weapons in Cuba, and on discovering this the United States asked for them to be removed. After intense negotiations between President John F Kennedy and the Soviet premier Nikita Khrushchev and their advisers and with the United Nations, the 'Cuban Missile Crisis' was averted. But for several crucial days, people all over the world contemplated the likelihood that they would be killed.

Regney's words were influenced by the sight of the mothers and babies in strollers who patrolled Manhattan's sidewalks. This was not an idealistic notion; the couple wrote the song at the very time that America was poised on the brink of war. Years later Shayne was to remark that when they had written the song neither she nor Regney were able to sing it all the way through. 'Our little song broke us up', she said, 'you must realize there was a threat of nuclear war at the time.'

The crisis was over when 'Do You Hear What I Hear' was released in America shortly after Thanksgiving in November 1962. Its first recording was made by the Harry Simeone Chorale who in 1958 had had a hit with 'The Little Drummer Boy'. Conceived as a 'B' side as it was, 'Do You Hear What I Hear' went on to sell more than a quarter of a million copies over the Christmas season. But it was Bing Crosby's version, recorded on Friday 22 November 1963 – the day that John F Kennedy was assassinated – that made it a worldwide hit.

Many artists since have recorded this song: Bob Dylan, Mahalia Jackson, Whitney Houston, Gladys Knight, Johnny Mathis and Andy Williams are just a few of them. It's a piece of music I didn't know as a child. It was introduced to me by the musical supervisor of *Songs of Praise* as a possible duet, a collaboration I could do with the boys' choir Libera, who were to perform it on *Songs of Praise*. I went into the studio to record it and was bowled over by the melody and the simplicity of the message. I've loved singing it. The most difficult thing in this carol is getting who said what to whom at exactly the right time. Our performance of 'Do

You Hear What I Hear' on *Songs of Praise* went down incredibly well. The whole idea I suppose that here was a man who was probably best known as a boy soprano singing, with young boys, a carol which is very simple and childlike in its creation, really did seem to resonate with the audience. I also love the fact that this carol builds up and up and up as the verses go along until 'Said the king to the people ev'rywhere / listen to what I say! / Pray for peace, people ev'rywhere'. It's glorious, it's the highlight of the carol and then all of a sudden you go back to why we're all there performing it with:

> The Child, the Child
> Sleeping in the night
> He will bring us goodness and light,
> He will bring us goodness and light.

It's almost like a Spielberg epic movie in the way it's been constructed. There are some really beautiful moments in it. From using your voice and your performance to portray 'A Star a star/Dancing in the night/ With a tail as big as a kite', but also a child, a child who shivers in the cold. It's built up to be very, very dramatic.

The power of this carol was further brought home to me a couple of years ago when my daughter, who was about seven years old at the time, came home from school having been told that she'd made it into the choir and the piece of music they were performing in the Christmas concert was 'Do You Hear What I Hear?' Just listening to the excitement in her voice, telling me the story of this carol and how she enjoyed singing it was just such a magical moment, which was further enhanced when I was asked by the school then to actually take the solo part myself. I'll never forget until my dying day glancing over and being winked at by my own daughter in the chorus while singing this carol.

GOD REST YOU MERRY, GENTLEMEN

WORDS
Anon.

MUSIC
'London', arranged by
John Stainer (1840–1901)

God rest you merry, gentlemen,
Let nothing you dismay,
For Jesus Christ our Saviour
Was born upon this day,
To save us all from Satan's power
When we were gone astray.

O tidings of comfort and joy,
Comfort and joy,
O tidings of comfort and joy.

In Bethlehem in Jewry
This blessed babe was born,
And laid within a manger
Upon this blessed morn;
The which his mother Mary
Nothing did take in scorn.

Refrain

From God our Heavenly Father
A blessed angel came,
And unto certain shepherds
Brought tidings of the same,
How that in Bethlehem was born
The Son of God by name.

Refrain

Fear not, then said the angel
Let nothing you affright,
This day is born a Saviour
Of virtue, power and might,
So frequently to vanquish all
The friends of Satan quite.

Refrain

The shepherds at those tidings
Rejoicéd much in mind,
And left their flocks a-feeding
In tempest, storm and wind,
And went to Bethlehem straightway
This blessed Babe to find.

Refrain

But when to Bethlehem they came,
Whereat this Infant lay,
They found him in a manger
Where oxen feed on hay;
His mother Mary kneeling
Unto the Lord did pray.

GOD REST
YOU MERRY,
GENTLEMEN

41

Refrain

Now to the Lord sing praises,
All you within this place,
And with true love and brotherhood
Each other now embrace;
This holy tide of Christmas
All others doth efface.

Refrain

The owner of one scant young nose, gnawed and mumbled by the hungry cold as bones are gnawed by dogs, stooped down at Scrooge's keyhole to regale him with a Christmas carol: but at the first sound of '*God bless you, merry gentlemen! May nothing you dismay!*', Scrooge seized the ruler with such energy of action, that the singer fled in terror, leaving the keyhole to the fog and even more congenial frost.

That word 'merry' expresses the uniquely jolly spirit of Christmas. Christmas is on its own as a festival of merrymaking as Dickens knew and conjured up in *A Christmas Carol* (1843) – of togetherness, warm fires, huge turkeys, well-laden tables and religious celebration – of 'comfort and joy' – which is exactly what 'God Rest You Merry' and carols in general were invented to express.

This is also another of those huge Christmas carols, probably one of the top five big ones that you expect to hear every Christmas. Of these Big Sing ones, and here I'm talking about 'O Come, All Ye Faithful', 'Hark! The Herald Angels Sing', 'The First Nowell', 'While Shepherds Watched Their Flocks by Night', I would say that 'God Rest You Merry, Gentlemen' is probably my favourite. It was a first for me in Bangor Cathedral. I remember being transfixed by the melody line. It's a massive carol from start to finish, and one that tells a story. The angel, the shepherds, they all make an entrance into this carol.

Its history is, as with so many carols, rather convoluted and sometimes controversial. It's generally agreed to be a folk carol, grown out of the rich carol tradition of the West of England, with its origins in the eighteenth or nineteenth century. Drawing on its West Country origins, William Sandys' *Christmas Carols, Ancient and Modern* (1833) is the main source for the version we sing today. Hugh Keyte and Andrew Parrott in their *New Oxford Book of Carols* offer us three tunes, the Sandys version as well as the 'London' tune, also known as 'Chestnut' in John Stainer's arrangement in *Christmas Carols New and Old* of 1871. Of John Stainer, Arthur Sullivan said bluntly, and memorably, 'He is a genius.' Stainer was an organist and composer, best known of course for his work *The Crucifixion*. He set high standards for Anglican church music, which are still influential today. He sang in the choir of St Paul's Cathedral, and I think there's a house in the choir school there that's still named after him. He became organist at Magdalen College, Oxford in 1860 and was made Professor of Music at Oxford in 1889. He was a prolific composer and his arrangements of 'God Rest You Merry, Gentlemen', as well as of 'The First Nowell' and 'I Saw Three Ships Come Sailing In', have become standard versions. Stainer died in Verona at the beginning of the twentieth century. His tune, Keyte and Parrott point out, has spawned many derivatives, including the melodies of 'While Shepherds Watched' and 'Here We Come A-wassailing'. Their third choice is from Ralph Dunstan's *Cornish Song Book* (1929), described by Dunstan rather vaguely as 'formerly popular in Cornwall'.

The question of the whereabouts of the comma in the first line of the carol has caused some confusion. As is so well demonstrated by Lynne Truss in *Eats Shoots and Leaves*, the placing of the comma can change the meaning entirely: in the hymn 'All Things Bright and Beautiful', 'The rich man in his castle, the poor man at his gate/God made them high or lowly' has a whole different meaning from 'The rich man in his castle, the poor man at his gate/God made them, high or lowly';

similarly, there's a different meaning between 'God Rest You, Merry Gentlemen' and the placing used widely today with the comma after 'Merry'. As Ian Bradley, in his excellent *The Daily Telegraph Book of Carols* (2006), observes, these words are probably addressed to the shepherds tending their flocks, telling them to fear not.

Through its life, 'God Rest You Merry' has given parodists pleasure. Its rhyme and rhythm, along with the first two lines, seem to offer these guys the ideal jumping-off point. Ian Bradley notes a parody of 1820, directed at Lord Castlereagh, then leader of the House of Commons, by the journalist William Hone (replacing that first-line comma):

> God rest you, merry Gentlemen,
> Let nothing you dismay;
> Remember we were left alive
> Upon last Christmas day,
> With both our lips at liberty
> To praise Lord C_____h,
> With his 'practical' comfort and joy!

Moving swiftly on, to American Jewish ace parodist Allan Sherman ('Hello Muddah, Hello Faddah . . .') and the song 'Schticks and Stones' in his album *My Son, the Folksinger*, which begins:

> 'God bless you, Jerry Mandelbaum may nothing you dismay;
> Dis May you had a rotten month, so what is there to say?
> Let's hope next May is better and good things will come your way
> And you won't have a feeling of dismay next May . . .'

Tom Lehrer's song 'A Christmas Carol' includes the line 'God rest ye merry merchants, may ye make the Yuletide pay . . .' and in 'Merry Christmas, Mr Bean', broadcast on Christmas Day 1992, Bean conducts a brass band, Bean-style, in a rendition of 'God Rest You Merry'.

In 2000, 'God Rest You Merry' didn't make it into the *Church Hymnary*, the hymnbook of the Church of Scotland. Along with 199 other 'traditional hymns and carols', including 'Jerusalem' and 'Stand Up, Stand Up for Jesus', 'God Rest You Merry' was declared by the Kirk to be out of tune with the twenty-first century. Urging modern worshippers to cast aside sentimental attachments, the committee's convener Revd John Bell said: 'There is something unjust if a church includes a hymn which only speaks to the past of those who are singing it and not to the future of those who are being born.' His objections to 'God Rest You Merry' included its exclusivity to the male gender, its archaisms and dubious theology, as well as its claim that 'This holy tide of Christmas/All others doth efface.' Well, in terms of gender, the alternative, 'God Rest You Merry, Gentlefolk', doesn't really work and to exclude according to the Revd Bell's latter point would be to excise quite a few other inspiring carols from the carol pantheon, including 'We Three Kings' and 'In the Deep Midwinter'. Anyway, undeterred, modern worshippers have voted with their voices and 'God Rest You Merry, Gentlemen' has remained a favourite, sixteenth in the 2005 *Songs of Praise* poll and lustily performed by carol singers at Christmastide.

The melody line of 'God Rest You Merry' creates a feeling of mystery. It's not obvious in any way, but it leaves a lasting impression on you when you sing it. It's also an unusual melody. Even though the first four lines are quite repetitive, it then goes somewhere totally different and is only brought back on line by the chorus, to a melodic line which gives the impression that you've heard it somewhere before, but you haven't. The melody line is incredibly strong as well, another Big Sing. You need a lot of energy to get through it. If it's sung in a lacklustre way, the refrain after every verse can be really tiresome. You need to keep that energy up and use body and soul to put across the message of 'Tidings of comfort and joy'.

Here is another carol with a terrific David Willcocks descant, which we used to sing in Bangor Cathedral, and the choir of Westminster Cathedral sing it in 'The Story of Christmas'. It's greatly enhanced by the involvement of the congregation. I am going to try and do this as a solo piece on my next Christmas album but God knows how it will turn out. I usually leave out the second verse in performance. So it's actually a six-verse carol that requires great stamina in the singing of it.

One thing I love about 'God Rest You Merry' is that coming together of the congregation, praising God in unison. At the final verse on the line, 'And with true love and brotherhood/Each other now embrace,' you always get people looking around at one another and there's a wonderful feeling of Christmas within either the church, chapel or concert hall where it's being performed.

10

O COME, O COME, EMMANUEL!

WORDS AND MUSIC
Eighth-century
Latin Advent Antiphons

TRANSLATION
John Mason Neale (1818–66)

O COME, O COME,
EMMANUEL!

O come, O come, Emmanuel!
And ransom captive Israel,
That mourns in lonely exile here
Until the Son of God appear.

47

Rejoice! Rejoice! Emmanuel
Shall come to thee, O Israel.

O come, Thou Rod of Jesse, free
Thine own from Satan's tyranny;
From depths of Hell Thy people save
And give them victory o'er the grave.

Refrain

O come, Thou day-spring, come and cheer
Our spirits by Thine advent here;
Disperse the gloomy clouds of night
And death's dark shadows put to flight.

Refrain

O come, o come, Emmanuel

VENI EMMANUEL
translated by J.M. Neale

Traditional

O come, Thou Key of David, come
And open wide our heavenly home;
Make safe the way that leads on high,
And close the path to misery.

Refrain

O come, O come, Thou Lord of Might,
Who to Thy tribes on Sinai's height
In ancient times did'st give the Law,
In cloud, and majesty, and awe.

Refrain

'O Come, O Come, Emmanuel!' is a very old work, probably our oldest Christmas carol, going right back to the eighth-century monasteries. It's a hymn for Advent, which was translated in the nineteenth century by the great hymnologist John Mason Neale from an old monastic psalter of that early period. The writer is unknown – probably a scholarly monk or priest with a deep knowledge of both Old and New Testaments. He designed its verses to be antiphons sung in Latin during vespers through the last seven days of Advent. One verse would have been chanted each day, and its words have in them that excitement of the anticipatory soul during the days and nights leading up to Christmas Eve.

'O Come, O Come, Emmanuel!' crosses biblical time, with the Old Testament predicting the events of the New. Somehow the carol collapses the ages that have passed between the prophecies and their fulfilment in the Incarnation. It's full of Old Testament images and references. Isaiah's prophecy (11:1) that the Messiah will be born into the line of King David's father Jesse, for example: 'a shoot will come up from the stump of Jesse; from his roots a Branch will bear fruit'. The Key of David comes again from Isaiah (22:22): 'And the key of the house of David will I lay upon his shoulder; so he shall shut, and none shall open'. It has a large and hopeful message, that the coming of Emmanuel (meaning 'God with us') will fulfil God's great promise to deliver us from the world. Musically it's not a typical carol, it's more religious-sounding melody-wise than all the others because of its background. The original chants of those monks can still be heard in the music of this song and its original words would have had great impact on the people of its times, who had little access to the Bible and its teachings. Its strong and spiritual nature has carried it through into modern days, modern audiences, and many languages.

John Mason Neale translated this Advent hymn as 'Draw nigh, draw nigh, Emmanuel' in 1851, then revising his translation to the version commonly sung today in 1853. Neale had taken orders in the Anglican church in 1841. He was high church in his sympathies and his Roman Catholic leanings were received with suspicion and some hostility. This may explain why he was never granted a pastorate in London – instead he was sent to the Madeira Islands and then in 1846 was allocated a lowly position as warden of Sackville College, an almshouse in East Grinstead. He never gave up on God or his calling though and in 1854 on an annual salary of just £27 he co-founded the Society of Saint Margaret, a female order of the Anglican Church, dedicated to nursing the sick. The Society continues today and is based in Boston, USA, where there are currently twenty-seven sisters, two dogs and five cats in the community. From this position he also established an orphanage, a school for girls and a refuge for prostitutes in East Grinstead.

Suffering in his life not only from religious opposition but also from ill health, Neale was nevertheless an energetic researcher who studied every Scripture-based writing he could find. It was while he was doing this research that he found the Latin chant 'Veni, veni, Emmanuel' in a book called the *Psalterium Cantionum Catholicorum*. Realising its importance, he immediately translated it into English and, put together with a fifteenth-century French Plainsong processional tune originating with a community of French Franciscan nuns living in Lisbon, it was published

initially in England in the 1850s. Later cut to five verses, 'O Come, O Come, Emmanuel!' grew and grew in popularity throughout Europe and America.

'O Come, O Come, Emmanuel!' has been covered by many artists, including Sufjan Stevens, Belle and Sebastian, Joan Baez and Enya. 2006's BBC Young Chorister of the Year William Dutton has also recorded it. In 2009 Bono, lead singer of U2, recorded a version of 'O Come, O Come, Emmanuel!' with new words and called it 'White As Snow'. It is written from the point of view of a soldier dying from a roadside bomb in Afghanistan. It is supposed to last the length of time it takes him to die. It has a quiet power and sadness that is true to the carol.

> Where I came from there were no hills at all
> The land was flat, the highway straight and wide.
> My brother and I would drive for hours
> Like we had years instead of days,
> Our faces as pale as the dirty snow . . .

I first came into contact with 'O Come, O Come, Emmanuel!' as a chorister at Bangor Cathedral, although we didn't sing it very often. My most vivid memory of this carol is that when I was performing *Strictly Come Dancing* a few years ago, I was also on tour, my largest tour ever. It was a Christmas tour around the British Isles, I think forty-seven concerts in fifty-two days, while also learning all my routines on *Strictly*. So during the day I would rehearse with my partner Lilia Kopolova for about seven hours wherever I was in the country and then that evening I would do a concert. Actually what was wonderful was that during the day, because I was so busy with the dancing, I wouldn't concentrate on the concert and then in the evening, when I was busy doing what I do best, which is singing, I wouldn't be thinking about the dancing. So each worked as an antidote to the other if you like.

I would start my Christmas tour with 'O Come, O Come, Emmanuel!' and such is the power of the piece of music that we started with the whole stage in darkness and I would sing the first verse offstage, unaccompanied. So all you would hear was the voice coming from nowhere: 'O Come, O Come, Emmanuel!/And ransom captive Israel'. And then during the second verse I would walk onto the stage and perform the rest of the carol. It worked a treat as a way to start a concert: you're asking God to join with you in what you're doing and the third verse in particular: 'Disperse the gloomy clouds of night/And death's dark shadows put to flight/Rejoice! rejoice! Emmanuel/shall come to thee, O Israel' banishes all negative thoughts, and what lies ahead – hopefully in the case of the concert I did – is a joyous celebration of Christmas music, which is exactly what it was. For me personally it was a great way of starting a concert because even though I had a string quartet and harp and guitar and piano and various other instruments and support artists – the lot – what I liked more than anything was that at the start you wouldn't even see the performer, all you heard was the voice and that was all that was important. And then my connection with the music didn't need any frills, didn't need any gimmicks. I just let the music stand for itself.

The reason why this carol is so popular is, I'd say, because it's a real dream to sing. It's an unusual melody line, not as simple as some of the other very well-known carols, which I've called childlike in this book. This is a lot more cultured as far as the melodic line is concerned and I think that's what adds to its mystery. I suppose that this is why it's not in the top five favourite carols, because it has that element of mystery and it's not obvious in any way.

11

GOOD KING WENCESLAS

WORDS
J M Neale (1818–66)

MUSIC
'Tempus Adest Floridum'
('It is time for flowering'): Anon.

GOOD KING
WENCESLAS

Good King Wenceslas looked out
On the feast of Stephen,
When the snow lay round about,
Deep and crisp and even;
Brightly shone the moon that night,
Though the frost was cruel,
When a poor man came in sight,
Gathering winter fuel.

'Hither, page, and stand by me,
If thou know'st it, telling,
Yonder peasant, who is he?
Where and what his dwelling?'
'Sire, he lives a good league hence,
Underneath the mountain,
Right against the forest fence,
By St. Agnes' fountain.'

'Bring me flesh, and bring me wine!
Bring me pine logs hither!
Thou and I will see him dine
When we bear them thither.'

53

Page and monarch, forth they went,
Forth they went together,
Through the rude wind's wild lament
And the bitter weather.

'Sire, the night is darker now
And the wind grows stronger;
Fails my heart I know not how,
I can go no longer.'
'Mark my footsteps, good my page,
Tread thou in them boldly:
Thou shalt find the winter's rage
Freeze thy blood less coldly.'

In his master's steps he trod
Where the snow lay dinted;
Heat was in the very sod
Which the saint had printed.
Therefore Christian men be sure,
Wealth or rank possessing,
Ye who now will bless the poor,
Shall yourselves find blessing.

'Good King Wenceslas' is as close to musical theatre as Christmas carols can get. I've performed it with the choir of Bangor Cathedral and it gives the boy soprano the opportunity to spit out the words, especially 'Deep and crisp and even', as well as 'Gathering winter fuel'. And then of course the men come in deep with 'Hither, page, and stand by me,/If thou know'st it, telling', hamming it up like mad and I've heard it done by many a cathedral choir who do the same sort of thing. It's almost as if with the serious Christmas carols like 'The Shepherds' Farewell' and others that really do need to be sung well, this is one you can get away with hamming it up a little bit.

As a young child I didn't really know what some of the words meant, but you know I always had a glint in the eye as did all my colleagues in Bangor Cathedral at the age of twelve when we used to sing:

> In his master's steps he trod
> Where the snow lay dinted;
> Heat was in the very sod
> Which the saint had printed.

It was later in life that I came to understand the true meaning of the words. The final verse which I've just referred to ends beautifully:

> Therefore Christian men be sure,
> Wealth or rank possessing,
> Ye who now will bless the poor,
> Shall yourselves find blessing.

There are some great descants by Derek Willcocks, which really set that last verse alight.

The life story of King Wenceslas himself (*c.* 907–935) is the stuff of fairy tales, complete with wicked family members. In fact Wenceslas, or Vaclav, to give him his native name, was not a king. For fourteen years, until he was murdered by his brother, he was Duke of Bohemia, now part of the Czech Republic. The poor chap was dubbed 'the father of all the wretched' by the Bohemian priest Cosmas of Prague. After his death, Otto the Great, Emperor of the Holy Roman Empire (912–973), is supposed to have conferred on him the grander title of king in recognition of his philanthropy, and he was canonised. His remains are still in Prague's St Vitus' Cathedral, where there are murals by a fifteenth-century Bohemian painter, the Master of the Litoměřice Altarpiece, that show Wenceslas distributing alms to the poor and working in the fields.

Wenceslas' father died when he was thirteen. He was brought up by his Christian grandmother Ludmilla – also to be canonised – who, with her husband the first Duke of Bohemia, converted Bohemia to Christianity. Drahomíra, the mother of Wenceslas and daughter of a pagan chief, may have tried to convert her son to paganism. Ludmilla thwarted her and, jealous of the power her mother-in-law had over her son, Drahomíra hired two assassins named Tunna and Gommon to murder Ludmilla. Legend has it that they strangled her with her own veil.

When Wenceslas came to power he sent his mother into exile as punishment, although he later reprieved her. This act of compassion did not lead to a family reunion. Instead in September 935, Wenceslas was killed on the orders of his brother, Boleslav, who had been brought up by Drahomíra. Boleslav repented and he promised he would educate his son, born on the day of his brother's murder, as a clergyman. This remorse may have been influenced by the displeasure of the Emperor Otto.

Our familiarity with the story of Wenceslas and with this festive and popular carol is down to the great hymnologist and writer John Mason Neale. In 1849 he published a fictional tale about the king and four years later followed it with the song.

In 1853 'Good King Wenceslas' was published in *Carols for Christmastide*, co-authored by Neale with the Reverend Thomas Helmore, musician and Vice-Principal of St Mark's College, Cambridge. It is likely that Neale had written the lyrics published there for 'Good King Wenceslas' at the same time as his story. This is one of eleven religious tales for children in a volume entitled *Deeds of Faith*.

The events of 'The Legend of Saint Wenceslaus' (the English spelling of his name) take place on Boxing Day. You really feel the cold in this story of personal sacrifice in the snow and freezing frost and it complements the Christmas story. On this day alms were distributed (probably in boxes) to the poor and gifts were given to tradespeople. The story opens with Wenceslas sitting at a window in his palace as the sun sets, dusk gathers and night falls. We can perhaps understand how the peace of watching the changing of day to night could help the king find connection to the workings of God.

By the light of a crescent moon Wenceslas spots a figure pulling at a bush in the snow and sends out his servant Otto to investigate. Otto reports back that Rudolph the swineherd is scratching for fuel for his cold and hungry family. Wenceslas tells Otto to fetch food and, much to Otto's horror for he thinks it's a job for servants, Wenceslas insists on carrying the wood himself. Otto refuses Wenceslas' offer to go to Rudolph's dwelling alone and heads off with him into the icy cold, copying his master's refusal to dress up warmly. Neale tells us that Wenceslas 'desired to feel with the poor, that he might feel for them'. Soon the servant is numb and can't walk. Wenceslas suggests he literally follow in his footsteps and Otto discovers that the ground where Wenceslas has trodden is warm with the 'fire of love that has kindled in him'. The king and his servant complete the journey and deliver the provisions.

Perhaps Neale felt some empathy with Wenceslas. He too lived by his principles. His devotion to high-church worship led to the restoration of his chapel (at his own expense) to include open benches, a cross, two candles and a rood screen and caused him to be 'inhibited' by his bishop for thirteen years. This meant the poor at the almshouse in Sussex, where he was warden for the last twenty years of his life, could not receive the sacraments. The Bishop of Chichester considered it his duty 'to stop Mr. Neale from continuing to debase the minds of the poor people with his spiritual haberdashery'. Only nine years after John Henry Newman had encouraged Roman Catholic practices in his church and then converted to Catholicism, Neale had aroused suspicions that he was an agent for the Vatican intent on destroying the Anglican Church.

In 1853 Neale and Thomas Helmore had been given a collection of Latin and Swedish songs, the *Piae Contiones* of 1582. It was a songbook that must have appealed to Neale, being a product of medieval Catholic culture. Some of the songs, such as 'Gaudete', are still popular. An English version of *Piae Contiones* was published in 1919 with a preface and notes by George Ratcliffe Woodward, the author of 'Ding Dong Merrily on High'. Oddly, given the chilly images conjured up by his lyrics, Neale chose the tune *'Tempus Adest Floridum'* ('It is time for flowering'), a thirteenth-century spring carol, to fit to his words.

There have been many recordings of 'Good King Wenceslas'. In 1963 it featured in several renditions on the first *Beatles Christmas Record*, with festive messages from the Fab Four. The disc lasted five minutes and ended with a chorus of 'Rudolph the Red-Nosed Ringo'. Joan Baez has recorded it, as have the Choir of King's College, Cambridge and Joan Sutherland with the New Philharmonia Orchestra. I recorded 'Good King Wenceslas' as a boy with the BBC Welsh Symphony Chorus on an album called *Aled Jones: The Christmas Album* in 1985.

Neale's story of the kindness and humility of a monarch is fiction. Little is known about Duke Vaclav of Bohemia although he is associated with many miracles and is now the patron saint of the Czech Republic. Nevertheless, it's the sentiment that counts and John Mason Neale wrote a tale and later a carol that dramatically illustrate an act of charity by a good king that still has the power to move us.

 **12**

HARK! THE HERALD ANGELS SING

WORDS
Charles Wesley (1707–88) and George Whitefield (1714–70)

MUSIC
Felix Mendelssohn (1809–47)

Arranged by W H Cummings (1831–1915)

Hark! the herald angels sing,
'Glory to the new-born King,
Peace on earth and mercy mild,
God and sinners reconciled.'
Joyful, all ye nations rise,
Join the triumph of the skies;
With th'angelic host proclaim:
'Christ is born in Bethlehem.'
Hark! the herald angels sing
'Glory to the new-born King.'

Christ, by highest Heaven adored,
Christ, the Everlasting Lord,
Late in time behold him come,
Offspring of a virgin's womb.
Veiled in flesh the Godhead see,
Hail the incarnate Deity!
Pleased as Man with man to dwell,

Jesus, our Emmanuel.
Hark! the herald angels sing
'Glory to the new-born King.'

Hail, the heaven-born Prince of Peace!
Hail, the Sun of Righteousness!
Light and life to all he brings,
Risen with healing in his wing.
Mild he lays his glory by,
Born that man no more may die,
Born to raise the sons of earth,
Born to give them second birth.
Hark! the herald angels sing
'Glory to the new-born King.'

What a double act! Words by Charles Wesley, music by Mendelssohn. You expect this carol to be world class and it is. 'Listen to those angels!' cries Wesley's 'Hymn for Christmas Day'. Mendelssohn's melody, soaring aloft, welcomes to earth Jesus our Emmanuel. Charles Wesley has left us a legacy of literally hundreds of fine hymns and at least two of his carols, 'Lo! He comes, with Clouds Descending' and 'Hark! The Herald Angels Sing' have remained great favourites. Wesley was an inspired craftsman, and a passionate poet, whose words to 'Hark! The Herald Angels Sing' display his deep conviction and his ability to wonder at the event of Christ's birth. His first hymn was written on the day of his conversion on 21 May 1738 and it opens 'Where shall my won'dring soul begin?'

Wesley's wonder had many forms; alongside his more serious works like 'Love Divine, All Loves Excelling' or 'Forth in Thy name, O Lord, I go/My daily labour to pursue', many of his poems celebrate mundane and earthly matters, like children teething, Handel's birthday or the courage of his cat:

I sing Grimalkin brave and bold
Who makes intruders fly
His claws and whiskers they behold
And squall and scamper by.

'Hark! The Herald Angels Sing' was first published in 1739 with the opening lines: 'Hark, how all the welkin rings / Glory to the King of Kings'. In 1779 John Wesley included it in his *A Collection of Hymns for the Use of the People Called Methodists*. At this time there was a new demand for hymns and it was the Methodists who brought them back into church services. Much to the annoyance of his elder brother John, then leader of the new Methodist movement started by Charles at Oxford, the poem was altered in 1753 by the Calvinistically inclined Methodist George Whitefield, whose advocacy of slavery the Wesley brothers opposed. He cut out two of the verses and substituted for Wesley's first lines the opening we sing today. Perhaps it was Whitefield that John was referring to when he grumbled that those who 'do my Brother and me (though without naming us) the honour of reprinting many of our hymns . . . are perfectly welcome to do so, provided they print them just as they are'. He proposed a solution, that these 'many gentlemen' print in the margin Charles's words, 'that we may no longer be held responsible either for the nonsense or the doggerel of other men'. Charles too was unlikely to have welcomed Whitefield's changes. More adjustments followed through the years. By the early nineteenth century 'Hark! The Herald Angels Sing' was usually sung in four-line stanzas. Then in the 1850s, the three or four verses were grouped together, each forming eight lines with a choral-type melody, to became the version we know today.

John Wesley wouldn't have approved of this modification:

Hark! The herald angels sing,
Beecham's Pills are quite the thing.
Two for a man and one for a child
Peace on earth and mercy mild.

Sir Thomas Beecham was a renowned conductor of the London Philharmonic Orchestra, but at one time the name Beecham was known in households for one reason only. Thomas's grandfather Joseph invented Beecham's powders, which made the family very rich. This wealth freed Thomas to pursue a career in music. Beecham's was one of the first businesses to grasp the value of advertising; nowadays sumo wrestlers convey strength of efficacy, but in the late 1800s, so it was rumoured, hymn books donated by Beecham's to a parish in South Shields carried the above rendition. This Joseph Beecham denied. Nevertheless, according to the National Archives, pedlars were hired to sing this version of 'Hark! The Herald Angels Sing' up and down Britain.

What gives any song the special quality that moves the singer and the listener is the dovetailing of a great tune with inspiring words. In the 1850s Wesley's words would find their perfect musical match. Dr William Hayford Cummings (1831–1915) began his singing career (as I did), when he was still a boy. Aged seven, he was a chorister at St Paul's Cathedral, and in his teens he was an organist at the Waltham Abbey parish church in Essex, where he wrote his arrangement of 'Hark! The Herald Angels Sing'. He had other talents; he wrote the first biography of Purcell, for instance, and he was an expert on Handel, but his obituary in the *Musical Times* remarked that as a 'composer he cannot be said to have made any special mark upon his generation'.

This perhaps unnecessary observation does not tell the whole story. Cummings has made an impression on many generations. One day in the 1850s he was flicking through Felix Mendelssohn's *Festgesang*, a work of four movements for male chorus. Mendelssohn had composed this as an occasional piece for the 1840 Gutenberg Festival in Leipzig celebrating the 400th anniversary of the invention of printing. Cummings was taken with a melody in the second movement, repeated in the fourth. He realised it would go with 'Hark! The Herald Angels Sing'. Mendelssohn had stipulated that his lively composition would be enjoyed by secular singers but was not suited to sacred words. Unaware of this, Cummings put Mendelssohn's music to Wesley's words and in 1856 the 'Hymn for

Christmas Day' we now sing was published. Inclusion in the first edition of *Hymns Ancient and Modern*, published in 1861 by a committee of clergy called the Proprietors, would seal this carol's happy partnership of lyrics and melody.

In 1885, the Revd James King set out to establish the Great Four Anglican Hymns in a survey of favourites conducted for his *Anglican Hymnology*. King attempted to arrive at the best ever hymn by gathering 52 hymn books from around the world and analysing their content using a weighting system of scores. He failed to find a number one: no hymn got a unanimous vote from all the books, but he did find four hymns that tied, with fifty-one 'votes' each. Two of them were by Charles Wesley: 'Lo! He Comes with Clouds Descending' and 'Hark! The Herald Angels Sing'.

Sir David Willcocks, King's College's Director of Music for seventeen years from 1957, made another adjustment to the carol – to its music this time. He introduced a harmonisation for the organ and a soprano descant for the last verse. This version is usually included in the Festival of Nine Lessons and Carols at King's College, Cambridge, where Dr Cummings, like Harold Darke, was once an organist. A recessional hymn, it is sung at the end when broadcasting has finished and the choir and clergy file out. David Willcock's descant is probably the greatest of its kind and probably David Willcock's own greatest descant. It's sublime and really does bring you closer to Heaven.

'Hark! The Herald Angels Sing' has been recorded by stars from outside the choral or classical world, such as Frank Sinatra, Johnny Cash and Mariah Carey. It is sung in the movie often shown during Christmas, Frank Capra's *It's a Wonderful Life* (1946), which, like carols themselves, celebrates the joy of living. And with discordant gusto the kids' choir belt through it in an episode of *South Park*.

Perhaps Charles and John Wesley, keen to see the right of worship and communication with God open to all, would have been gratified to witness the power of this carol to move millions nearly three centuries after its original publication.

I sang this carol first with gusto when I was at primary school, then with a little bit more finesse when I was in Bangor Cathedral Choir. It's the carol equivalent of a hymn like 'Guide Me Oh Thou Great Redeemer', in the way that you need quite a lot of stamina to get through it. It's a big sing, a big ask, a big commitment. It starts on full power and then builds to even greater glory throughout every verse. Used very often as a recessional, during our Nine Lessons and Carols we do exactly that in our charity performance in St George's Hanover Square and I'm always literally cream crackered by the time I get to the back door of the church, having let rip during this one.

I may be castigated for saying this, but I really do think this carol is at its best when it's performed by a full cathedral choir to the glorious organ accompaniment. I've recorded it as a solo artist with choir accompaniment and it does work even then, just probably not as well. I didn't record it as a child – unbelievably. I don't know whether it's because of my chorister background, but whenever I see this hymn on a sheet now at a service or at a charity event, my heart sinks a little bit because it is an incredibly difficult sing. As I've said, you really do need to have lungs of steel and also a major amount of stamina. This isn't something you can come to lightly, you've got to give your all, vocally, body and soul when you perform 'Hark! The Herald Angels Sing'.

13

O HOLY NIGHT

WORDS   MUSIC
Placide Clappeau (1808–77)   Adolphe Charles Adam (1803–56)

O holy night! The stars are brightly shining,
It is the night of the dear Saviour's birth.
Long lay the world in sin and error pining,
Till He appeared, gift of infinite worth.
A thrill of hope, a weary world rejoices,
For yonder breaks a new and glorious morn,
Fall on your knees! Oh, hear the angel voices!
Oh night divine, O night when Christ was born;
O night, O holy night, O night divine!

Led by the light of faith serenely beaming,
With glowing hearts by His cradle we stand.
O'er the world a star is sweetly gleaming,
Now come the wise men from the Orient land.
The King of kings lay thus in lowly manger;
In all our trials born to be our friend.
He knows our need, our weakness is no stranger,
Behold your King! Before him lowly bend!
Behold your King! Before him lowly bend!

Truly He taught us to love one another,
His law is love and His gospel is peace.
Chains he shall break, for the slave is our brother

O HOLY
NIGHT

65

O holy night

Placide Capeau
translated by J.S. Dwight

Adolphe Adam

And in His name all oppression shall cease.
Sweet hymns of joy in grateful chorus raise we,
With all our hearts we praise His holy name.
Christ is the Lord! Then ever, ever praise we,
His power and glory ever more proclaim!
His power and glory ever more proclaim!

'O Holy Night' is by way of being a paradox. It is the most beautiful of carols, composed by the man who wrote the flowing music for the ballet *Giselle* and written by a French poet. It came in at fourth place in the 2005 BBC *Songs of Praise* poll and its place in the hearts of people who love carols is assured. But, but, 'O Holy Night' is not often sung by congregations in church services and is a rarity in books of hymns and carols. It's a gift to a solo performer and you are more likely to hear it crooned by balladeers Nat 'King' Cole and Perry Como, or recorded in the US by country music singers like Martina McBride or John Berry. It's a favourite with opera stars: Joan Sutherland and Luciano Pavarotti have given the carol memorable renditions and Welsh mezzo-soprano Katherine Jenkins shattered a glass chandelier above her head while singing it recently.

Nevertheless, this carol has frequently been kept outside the church door. This is not unusual in the life stories of carols. Churchmen have often suspected that they are not quite religiously respectable. You can find a few more instances of this in my choice for this book, where carols with pagan origins or those accused of political incorrectness come up, and occasionally with carols that do not mention Christ himself. So why is this most religious of songs, which considers the birth of Jesus and the redemption of human beings, seen by some as an undesirable at Christmas? In this instance, the answer could lie in the tendency of carols to reflect the tenor of their times; a few of our most famous carols do express coded opinions on contemporary events: 'O Come, All Ye Faithful', for example. One answer lies perhaps in the third line of the third

stanza: 'Chains he shall break, for the slave is our brother/And in His name all oppression shall cease.'

Placide Clappeau, who wrote the poem '*Minuit, Chrétiens*' on which 'O Holy Night' is based, was a freethinker. He was raised in the small town of Roquemaure, near Avignon in the Rhone Valley, and in a region where wine is a religion, he was destined to follow in his father's footsteps into the wine business. But a painful event changed the direction of his life. When he was eight years old, he was accidentally shot in the hand by a friend. His hand was amputated and, thus disabled, he changed direction to study hard and gain a literature degree in Paris. While earning his living in the wine trade, he was also writing poetry, as well as being the mayor of Roquemaure.

But Placide also had socialist, republican and anti-clerical leanings. Like other nineteenth-century creators of carols, from Charles Wesley to Christina Rossetti, he was opposed to slavery and the slave trade that supported the prosperity of his country. This slipped into a line of his poem.

Another reason why 'O Holy Night' has not found its way into many hymnals could be that both Placide Clappeau and its composer, Adolphe Adam, had their reputations attacked by churchmen in their native France for being unbelievers. It's been claimed that Adam was in fact Jewish and Clappeau was of course damned as a freethinking radical. The story goes that on 3 December 1847 Clappeau was about to embark upon a business trip to Paris when the local parish priest asked him to write a Christmas poem. About halfway to Paris, Clappeau apparently became inspired and wrote the poem, '*Minuit, Chrétiens*' or 'O Holy Night'. When Clappeau arrived in Paris, he asked a friend of a friend, Adolphe Charles Adam, to compose a tune for it. Adam had studied at the Paris Conservatoire and was then at the height of his career as a composer of comic opera. His operas, like *Le Postillon de Lonjumeau* and *Si j'étais roi* are hardly known today, but his ballet *Giselle* is famous. He'd also written songs for the Paris vaudeville and earned his living as organist. He'd even played the triangle in the orchestra of the Conservatoire. He wrote the tune to

Clappeau's poem in a few days and 'Cantique de Noël' received its first performance at midnight mass in Roquemaure parish church on Christmas Eve 1847. Adam later called their carol 'la Marseillaise religieuse': the religious national anthem of France. Despite resistance from the French clergy, the carol was a success, first in France and then abroad after it had been published in an English version in 1855. Its beauty had won the day.

'O Holy Night' is treasured in the United States, thanks to John Sullivan Dwight's translation (1812–93), which has become the standard version. Dwight was a Harvard graduate, Unitarian minister for 6 years then a music journalist and critic. He edited Dwight's Journal of Music for 30 years and lived most of his life in and around Boston and made a home at the Transcendentalist community of Brook Farm, Massachusetts. Like Clappeau, he held strong anti-slavery views and perhaps that is why he was drawn to this carol and translated it so sensitively.

Two, apocryphal, stories about this carol are worth telling. The first is that it figured prominently on Christmas Eve in 1870 during the Franco-Prussian War. Apparently a French soldier suddenly and unexpectedly jumped out of the trench and sang 'O Holy Night'. Instead of firing at him, his German adversaries sang a German carol (reputedly Martin Luther's 'Vom Himmel hoch, da komm' ich her', 'From Highest Heaven I Come to Tell') in response. The other, short, story is that 'O Holy Night' was the first ever music performed live on radio. It was broadcast by Reginald Fessenden who played the tune on his violin for ships at sea on 24 December 1906 from his radio station in Massachusetts.

I first got to perform 'O Holy Night' when I went out to Israel as a boy soprano. I was recording three programmes for BBC1, two for Easter, one for Christmas, and I was dressed up in my cassock and ruff from my cathedral, and when it came to recording 'O Holy Night' I was actually going to be miming to the music I had recorded in Cardiff, but in all the relevant holy places in Israel. I remember 'O Holy Night' was being sung/mimed to in the exact spot where Jesus was born in Bethlehem. I think it's called the Church of the Nativity and it's really a cave. What an honour to be performing in this place. But there's a story that goes with it. I was out in Israel with the BBC Welsh Chorus and they'd finished work for the day so they were going back to the kibbutz to swim, but unfortunately I had to go and do the 'O Holy Night' performance. So there was a part of me that wanted to get it done as soon as possible so I could jump in the pool with the whole chorus who were having a whale of a time. But also it was incredibly warm everywhere we were filming in Israel. On TV you see me dressed in cassock and ruff. You'd think that what I was wearing underneath was a shirt and tie and smart pair of trousers but all I was actually wearing was a pair of shorts, not even a top, such was the heat.

It's a carol that's meant the world to me ever since then and it's actually the carol that brought me back to singing as a man. I was asked to perform it on *Songs of Praise* and I went down to the home of Robert Prizeman, who's the programme's music supervisor, and we recorded the adult version of 'O Holy Night' specially for the *Songs of Praise* performance. Well, Robert also had my boy soprano recording there and he played both at exactly the same time. It was uncanny: the voice, the phrasing and the interpretation of the piece were *exactly* the same as a man as they had been when I was a boy. So this gave me hope, if you like, that I could be a professional singer again. The feeling and emotion I had as a boy had come back to me as a man. I'd done musicals and quite a few concerts but the joy I had of singing as a boy, the instinctive joy, had not been there as an adult but came back with this piece, 'O Holy Night'.

Since then I've sung 'O Holy Night' in concert many times and I've even been back to Israel to perform it again. It's able to move an audience greatly. One performance I did on *Songs of Praise* was filmed by a really talented producer called Medwin Hughes who had the idea of starting with me as a boy singing that carol in the cave in Bethlehem, and then zooming out to me in a live concert situation performing it – I think at Birmingham Symphony Hall – as a man. There is a part where the young Aled is singing with the slightly older and fatter Aled. And the feedback

that came when that programme went out was so strong: people really, really loved it. So it's a carol I've had associations with since I was a very very small boy.

'O Holy Night' is a joyous carol to perform, the words and music complement each other beautifully. Lines such as 'A thrill of hope, a weary world rejoices/For yonder breaks a new and glorious morn/Fall on your knees! . . .' are very dramatic; looking back, my performance as a boy in the cave in Bethlehem was also rather dramatic and I remember feeling quite embarrassed that I had my hands clasped together giving it my all. It's a carol that requires you to be positive and you need to give everything you've got when you're performing it.

It's funny, sometimes some carols work better than others on stage in a concert scenario, and this is one that really does work. You can end a Christmas concert easily with 'O Holy Night'. It's that powerful and I suppose for me it's a carol that will always take me back to those early days in Israel; how fortunate I was to be singing in the actual place where Jesus was born. This beautiful carol tells that story, so having the opportunity to sing it in the exact spot was a real honour.

O HOLY
NIGHT

71

14

IN THE BLEAK MIDWINTER

Words
Christina Rossetti (1830–94)

Music
Gustav Holst (1874–1934),
Harold Darke (1888–1976)

Aled Jones'
favourite
christmas carols

72

In the bleak midwinter
Frosty wind made moan,
Earth stood hard as iron,
Water like a stone;
Snow had fallen, snow on snow,
Snow on snow,
In the bleak midwinter,
Long ago.

Our God, heaven cannot hold him
Nor earth sustain;
Heaven and earth shall flee away
When he comes to reign:
In the bleak mid-winter
A stable-place sufficed
The Lord God almighty,
Jesus Christ.

Enough for him, whom cherubim
Worship night and day,
A breastful of milk
And a mangerful of hay;

Enough for him, whom angels
Fall down before,
The ox and ass and camel
Which adore.

Angels and archangels
May have gathered there,
Cherubim and seraphim
Thronged the air;
But only his mother
In her maiden bliss
Worshipped the Beloved
With a kiss.

What can I give him,
Poor as I am?
If I were a shepherd
I would bring a lamb;
If I were a wise man
I would do my part
Yet what I can give him,
Give my heart.

'In the Bleak Midwinter' has been in my soul since I was nine years old when I first sang it in Bangor Cathedral as a probationer. This carol is not a cheery offering to accompany mince pies and mulled wine; Christina Rossetti's words provoke a sombre mood. Her poem 'A Christmas Carol' appeared (with odd timing) in the January 1872 edition of the American magazine *Scribner's Monthly*. *Scribner's'* editor advertised the poem, somewhat coyly, as 'a little poem in my breast-pocket – wise in a sort of child-wisdom, sweet and clear and musical as the sunset chimes . . . yes, and cheerier, for it celebrates that first Christmas morning.'

Still, he paid Christina the liberal fee of £10 for her little poem.

There are certain carols that when you hear them really do get you in the mood for Christmas. The minute you hear 'In the Bleak Midwinter' it's as if a warm glow comes over you and you eagerly anticipate the great event. Rossetti's choice of title perhaps evoked the warmth of Charles Dickens' story of Scrooge and the Cratchit family, written for Christmas 1843. Dickens' novella had a purpose – to rejuvenate the old Christmas traditions that people had enjoyed before Cromwell's icy hand cancelled Christmas celebrations. New customs were coming in for Christmas in his and Christina Rossetti's time; sending greetings cards, for instance, or dressing the Christmas tree while outside the window snow lay deep and crisp and even. There is something very Dickensian in this carol. It perfectly sets the scene for Christmas. You feel safe when you're singing it; that all is good in the world for those three very special minutes.

Christina Rossetti was born 20 days before Christmas 1830, described by her father Gabriele as having a round face, 'like a little moon risen at the full'. She grew up in a close and loving Italian family. Her father was a poet and political exile, who had fled from the kingdom of Naples with a price on his head. Her younger brother, the poet and painter Dante Gabriel, was a leading member of the Pre-Raphaelite Brotherhood. Her mother Frances, full of 'commonsense and modesty', was a devout Anglo-Catholic, and Christina was also deeply religious. This shy woman was in her life and her work a brave protagonist. She opposed slavery, rescued prostitutes and was active in the movement for animal rights. She was also a visionary poet. Virginia Woolf wrote of her, 'Modest you were, still you were drastic, sure of your gift, convinced of your vision.' Christina Rossetti died as she was born, close to Christmas, on 29 December 1894, of cancer.

Rossetti takes poetic licence by placing Christ's birth in a wintry landscape, white with deep snow. There's a big pile of hay in the stable, enough for the traditional ox and the ass – and a camel for good measure. She had an unrivalled ear for music, but she did not intend either 'A Christmas Carol' or her 1885 'Christmastide' (which became the carol

'Love came down at Christmas') to be set to music as carols. The free rhythm of her poem wasn't considered easy to set to music, but there are two memorable arrangements for it. Gustav Holst put Rossetti's words to music for *The English Hymnal* of 1906. Holst, whose astrologically inspired orchestral suite *The Planets* gave him the celebrity he loathed, was, like Rossetti, a poorly child and adult. He was a little accident-prone as well – in 1923 he suffered concussion having fallen backwards off his podium. Again like Rossetti though, neither ailment nor accident could sap his creative energy and he continued to teach and compose up to his death in 1934. The piece he wrote for Rossetti's poem is called 'Cranham' after the village outside Cheltenham from which his mother's family came. The little house where he wrote it is now fittingly called 'Midwinter Cottage'. His simple, evocative tune must take its share of credit for the popularity of this carol.

Harold Darke wrote his music to Rossetti's poem three years after Holst when he was just twenty-one and a student at the Royal College of Music. Born in London, he was an organist by profession. He was organist at the Church of St Michael, Cornhill in the City of London for a good fifty years and while at Cornhill he gave over 1,800 organ recitals at Monday lunchtimes for an enthusiastic audience. This, the Cornhill Lunchtime Organ Recitals series that he began in 1916, is the longest running of its kind in the world, and continues to flourish today with Jonathan Rennert the current organist. One of the things I love about the Darke music for 'In the Deep Midwinter' is its beautiful, delicate organ accompaniment. He also seems effortlessly to have met the rhythmical challenges of Rossetti's poem.

Recently, Bob Chilcott, formerly a member of the King's Singers, has written a choral setting for 'In the Bleak Midwinter' called simply 'Midwinter'. His version was, I expect, brought to prominence by the King's College Choir because they sing it in their Nine Lessons and Carols, broadcast to millions around the world each year. Fitting to its origins this, because Harold Darke was himself a conductor of the choir during the Second World War.

'In the Bleak Midwinter' has twice been voted a Christmas number one. In 2005 it knocked 'Silent Night' off the top spot in a *Songs of Praise* poll. In 2008, Darke's arrangement was judged favourite of the UK and US music directors who contributed to the *BBC Music Magazine* poll.

I was at once struck by the sheer perfection of this carol. It's definitely one of my top three favourites of all time and what's testament to this carol is that I like the melody by Holst and the one by Darke equally. Recently the *Songs of Praise* producer managed very cleverly to put on a performance I was involved in at the Royal Albert Hall (it's always in the Royal Albert Hall – always the Big Sing!) where we incorporated both melodies. They have similarities and were of course composed really close together in time. The congregation sang the first couple of verses to the Darke melody and then yours truly was to take the solo in the third verse to the Holst melody. Well, I was the only one who managed to mess it up because in the middle of the Holst, I crept into the Darke melody, which is very easily done. And this carol will be included on my new album at Christmas, probably the Holst melody this time round all the way through.

This is a carol that takes you on a journey where you can really use every aspect of colour in your voice and performance. It's almost like a theatrical carol. You're setting the scene in the first verse, where the earth is hard, water's like a stone, winds are moaning and snow is falling, not just a little, but snow on snow, snow on snow. It's like the first chapter in a Harry Potter book, you just want to read on to find out what happens next!

The most lyrical of the verses is the third. It's the one where the singer in you can really come out. It's full of rhythm changes from 'In the bleak midwinter/Frosty wind made moan' to, in the third verse:

> Enough for him, whom cherubim
> Worship night and day,
> A breastful of milk
> And a mangerful of hay;

Enough for him, whom angels
Fall down before,
The ox and ass and camel,
Which adore.

This is just a different rhythm, which falls beautifully within the voice. The fourth verse is usually missed out in my performances anyway, so I go from verses one, two and three into the final 'What can I give him/ Poor as I am?' I know people love singing this carol; I do anyway. Because it's a fantastic sing, it's a beautiful melody, wonderful words, but also the final verse brings it all back to being humble – the fact that if you were a shepherd you'd have given one of your flock, if a wise man you'd have done your part, but all you can give is your heart. This is reinforced right the way through the carol. If you sing it with honesty and an open heart, you can't go wrong.

I've performed 'In the Deep Midwinter' so many times. It's a crowd pleaser but also a performer pleaser. There are so many of these carols that I sing to hopefully make an audience smile but also because I absolutely love singing them.

15

IT CAME UPON
THE MIDNIGHT CLEAR

WORDS
Edmund Hamilton Sears (1810–76)

MUSIC
Richard Storrs Willis (1819–1900),
Arthur Sullivan (1842–1900)

78

It came upon the midnight clear,
That glorious song of old,
From angels bending near the earth
To touch their harps of gold:
'Peace on the earth, good will to men,
From heaven's all-gracious King!'
The world in solemn stillness lay
To hear the angels sing.

Still through the cloven skies they come,
With peaceful wings unfurled;
And still their heavenly music floats
O'er all the weary world:
Above its sad and lowly plains
They bend on hovering wing;
And ever o'er its Babel-sounds
The blessed angels sing.

Yet with the woes of sin and strife
The world has suffered long;
Beneath the angel-strain have rolled
Two thousand years of wrong;
And man, at war with man, hears not
The long-song which they bring:
O hush the noise, ye men of strife,
And hear the angels sing.

And ye, beneath life's crushing load,
Whose forms are bending low,
Who toil along the climbing way
With painful steps and slow,
Look, now! For glad and golden hours
Come swiftly on the wing;
O rest beside the weary road
And hear the angels sing.

For lo! the days are hastening on,
By prophet-bards foretold,
When, with the ever-circling years,
Comes round the age of gold;
When peace shall over all the earth
Its ancient splendours fling,
And the whole world give back the song
Which now the angels sing.

Edmund Sears wrote this powerful anthem for peace in December 1849 four months before his fortieth birthday. In his *Sermons and Songs of the Christian Life*, Sears places 'It Came Upon the Midnight Clear' right after his sermon based on the biblical text Hebrews 12:1 concerning the doctrine of angels:

Seeing we also are compassed about with so great a cloud of witnesses, let us lay aside every weight, and the sin which doth so easily beset us, and let us run with patience the race that is set before us . . .

His great cloud of witnesses, the multitude of the Heavenly host, take centre-stage here and carry the Christmas message of peace on earth, good will to men. They are wonderfully bird-like, dynamic angels: 'Still through the cloven skies they come/with peaceful wings unfurled . . . They bend on hovering wing'.

Edmund Hamilton Sears was born in 1810 in Sandisfield, Massachusetts. The town was founded upon a rural economy, and when they tried to introduce other industries, these failed when a planned railway line fell through. Perhaps growing up in a township so recently settled, Sears was aware of the fragility that such a community has. He was brought up on a farm, the youngest of three boys, and chose to become a Unitarian minister.

At the time he wrote this carol Sears was a pastor in Wayland, Massachusetts. 'It Came Upon the Midnight Clear' was published in the *Christian Register* of 29 December 1849. Then in 1850 Sears asked his friend, the American composer Richard Storrs Willis to set his words to music. The resulting composition is called 'Carol' and in 1875 it appeared in Sears' *Sermons and Songs of the Christian Life*, in which he reminds us that our lives are witnessed, we do not act in isolation or unobserved: 'Your home may be humble, apart, alone; but if a good life is lived there, it stands in the centre of an amphitheatre thronged with heavenly multitudes, all bending towards you and breathing their spirit into yours.'

The social message carried in these verses was in line with Sears' faith and with the Unitarian church's anti-war sentiments. Because Unitarianism teaches belief in the sole personality of God, rather than the doctrine of the Trinity, the words in this poem do not describe the birth of Christ or make Christological references. This might have meant

it was easier for those Unitarians who did not view Jesus as divine to sing it. However Sears himself believed in the divinity of Jesus and 'Calm on the Listening Ear of Night', the carol for which he is also known, does have the Nativity at its centre. It is still popular in America, though not often sung in the UK.

Like Gloria Shayne and Noel Regney, the writers of 'Do You Hear What I Hear?', Sears wrote 'It Came upon the Midnight Clear' for a world in which prospects for peace seemed threatened to be eclipsed by the savagery of war. It is sometimes suggested that he was influenced by the revolutions in Europe at that time and by a recent war between America and Mexico between 1846 and 1848 over right of possession of Texas. But unlike 'Do You Hear What I Hear?', Sears' poem makes a direct call to humanity to 'hush the noise' and to live in peace with one another.

Sears first preached the sermon that precedes his poem 'Carol' in 1865 at the end of the American Civil War which had raged since 1861. He would have been mindful of 'the thousands of martyrs, the flower of the country' who gave up their lives. It was a time when, after so many casualties, the value of peace would have been held high in the hearts of his congregation.

In the UK 'It Came upon the Midnight Clear' is sung to a different melody. Arthur Sullivan, one half of Gilbert and Sullivan, reworked a traditional carol from Herefordshire that was reportedly sent to him by a friend. It was likely that Sullivan, himself an agnostic, was attracted to Sears' humanist Unitarianism. His tune was titled 'Eardisley', after the Herefordshire town (it is also known as 'Noel'), and the resulting arrangement was published in *Church Hymns* in 1874 with the credit: 'Traditional Air rearranged'.

When this carol was first published in Britain, in Edward Bickersteth's *Hymnal Companion to the Book of Common Prayer* of 1870, it underwent changes that give it a more Christocentric feel. Bickersteth took out the third verse and rewrote the fifth as follows:

For lo the days are hastening on,
By prophets seen of old,
When with the ever-circling years
Shall come the time foretold,
When the new heaven and earth shall own
The Prince of Peace their King,
And the whole world send back the song
Which now the angels sing.

Then in the next century Erik Routley's 1961 *University Carol Book* changes the last five lines of this new version to:

Came round the day foretold,
When men, surprised by joy, adored
The prince of peace, their king;
Come all who hear! Join in the song
Which men and angels sing.

So, as with many carols and hymns, this song with its powerful melody and words that move us has come on a journey to become what we sing today, but over the last hundred and sixty years its core message has remained unchanged. Christ's coming is of course a time to celebrate, but Sears' words ask us to remember that this time it signals a call to service. The angels have witnessed two thousand years of conflict among humanity: 'It Came upon the Midnight Clear' voices their plea for peace on earth and challenges us to listen and to take responsibility to stop our wars.

 **16**

JESUS CHRIST THE APPLE TREE

WORDS   MUSIC
Anon.   Elizabeth Poston (1905–87)

The tree of life my soul hath seen,
Laden with fruit and always green:
The trees of nature fruitless be
Compared with Christ the apple tree.

His beauty doth all things excel:
By faith I know, but ne'er can tell,
The glory which I now can see
In Jesus Christ the apple tree.

For happiness I long have sought,
And pleasure dearly I have bought:
I missed of all; but now I see
'Tis found in Christ the apple tree.

I'm weary with my former toil,
Here I will sit and rest awhile:
Under the shadow I will be,
Of Jesus Christ the apple tree.

This fruit doth make my soul to thrive,
It keeps my dying faith alive:
Which makes my soul in haste to be
With Jesus Christ the apple tree.

JESUS CHRIST THE
APPLE TREE

83

This carol was introduced to me by J Mervyn Williams and Hefen Owen, producers of most of my albums as a boy. Invariably I'd meet up with the organist that was going to accompany me on my albums on the morning of the recording and I remember them saying, 'How do you feel about recording this album?' Well, I'd never heard this one before. But after going through it a couple of times with the organist I knew it was something I could do justice to.

The mysterious lyrics of the piece are by an American author who remains unknown. He or she was probably living in New England in the 1700s as the lyrics first appeared in *Divine Hymns, or Spiritual Songs: for the use of Religious Assemblies and Private Christians* published in 1784 by Joshua Smith, a lay Baptist minister from New Hampshire. Apple trees were grown widely in New England and this might have provided the inspiration for the song, or maybe the lyrics are a meditation on the verses from the Song of Songs (2:3): 'As the apple tree among the trees of the wood, so is my beloved among the sons. I sat down under his shadow with great delight, and his fruit was sweet to my taste.'

The setting of the carol I used to sing is by Elizabeth Poston, who is a twentieth-century English composer born on 24 October 1905 at Pin Green, Stevenage. Her father died in 1914 when Elizabeth was nine. Her mother Clementine then took her and her brother to live at Rooks Nest House, which was also the childhood home of E M Forster, who lived there between 1883 and 1893. It's the house on which Howards End, the setting for Forster's novel of the same name, is based. Elizabeth Poston lived at Rooks Nest House for the rest of her life, and in a neat connection, it was there that she wrote the score for the 1970 television production of Forster's novel.

Both Peter Warlock and Ralph Vaughan Williams mentored Elizabeth Poston during her studies at the Royal Academy of Music in London. She travelled during the 1930s studying architecture and during her travels she, like her mentor Vaughan Williams, collected folk songs. She came back to England at the beginning of the Second World War and began a new career in radio broadcasting for the BBC, becoming Director of Music in the European Service.

During the war Elizabeth Poston went underground, working for the British Government using gramophone records to send coded messages to allies in Europe. She never revealed the exact nature of this work and it remains secret to this day. Poston had a role in the creation of the BBC Third Programme, which became Radio 3 and between 1955 and 1961 she was the president of the Society of Women Musicians.

Her melody is enchanting to sing and is ideally suited to a boy chorister's voice. It's very much in the same vein as 'Once in Royal David's City' in being very exposed but also giving opportunities to really soar with the melodic line. I recorded it on my Christmas album back in 1985 as a boy soprano. It was a favourite of Robert Runcie, the 102nd Archbishop of Canterbury; actually I think it was sung at his funeral. Poston's setting is in the key of C major and there aren't any accidentals in the score so it gives it a really folk-song-like sound, very pure and also means you can put your own stamp on it: there's no strict metre, you can play around with the time, which gives you carte blanche on performance. And that's what I used to love about it, the blank sheet. When I sat there with the organist that morning we were able very, very quickly to create something I was proud of. I'll record it as an adult as well and hopefully I will be as lucky this time round. Such is the melody of 'Jesus Christ the Apple Tree' that I used to sing the first couple of verses unaccompanied, I've even sung it all unaccompanied. It doesn't need an organ accompaniment, or strings, or anything gimmicky. All one needs is the purity of the voice and the passion of the performance.

O little town of Bethlehem

P. Brooks

17

O LITTLE TOWN OF BETHLEHEM

WORDS Phillips Brooks (1835–93)

MUSIC 'Forest Green' by Ralph Vaughan Williams (1872–1958),
'Wengen' by Henry Walford Davies (1869–1941)

O little town of Bethlehem,
How still we see thee lie!
Above thy deep and dreamless sleep
The silent stars go by.
Yet in thy dark streets shineth
The everlasting light,
The hopes and fears of all the years
Are met in thee tonight.

O morning stars, together
Proclaim the holy birth,
And praises sing to God the King,
And peace to men on earth;
For Christ is born of Mary,
And, gathered all above,
While mortals sleep, the angels keep
Their watch of wondering love.

How silently, how silently,
The wondrous gift is given!
So God imparts to human hearts

The blessings of his heaven.
O holy child of Bethlehem,
No ear may hear his coming;
But in this world of sin,
Where meek souls will receive him, still
The dear Christ enters in.

Where children pure and happy
Pray to the blessed child,
Where misery cries out to thee,
Son of the mother mild;
Where charity stands watching
And faith holds wide the door,
The dark night wakes, the glory breaks,
And Christmas comes once more.

O holy child of Bethlehem
Descend to us we pray;
Cast out our sin and enter in,
Be born in us today.
We hear the Christmas angels
The great glad tidings tell:
O come to us, abide with us,
Our Lord Emmanuel.

On Christmas Eve 1865, Phillips Brooks, an American Episcopalian priest, stood in the field outside Bethlehem where the angel of the Lord is said to have appeared to the shepherds. He had taken a year's leave of absence from his Holy Trinity Church in Philadelphia to do a world tour and, stopping off in Jerusalem, he picked up a horse and rode it from there to Bethlehem. He was deeply moved by his moments in this field and by the five-hour service in Bethlehem

at the Church of the Nativity on the supposed site of Jesus' birth. He said,

> I remember standing in the old church in Bethlehem close to the spot where Jesus was born, when the whole church was ringing hour after hour with splendid hymns of praise to God, how again and again it seemed as if I could hear voices I knew well, telling each other of the *Wonderful Night* of the Savior's birth.

Later, in 1868, after returning home to Philadelphia and drawing on this experience, he wrote 'O Little Town of Bethlehem' for the children of his Sunday School to sing at Christmas.

Phillips conveys beautifully the quiet streets of a small town in the middle of the night. Unusually in the writing of carols, which tend to trumpet their celebrations, this one is gentle and dwells on the contrast between the hushed setting and the wondrous thing that is happening there. He gave his verses to his organist, Lewis Redner, asking him to compose a tune for it. Lewis couldn't, try as he might, find the melody, but the night before Christmas he woke with the music 'ringing in my ears, full formed and harmonized'. He jotted the notes down and went back to sleep. The tune is called 'St Louis' after him and it is still the standard one in the US.

Phillips Brooks was born in Boston. He was over six foot six, a man of great physical presence and spiritual strength. When giving sermons, his delivery came in lightning bursts – it's said that he spoke at a rate of over 200 words a minute; one wonders how his congregation kept up! He was also a committed humanitarian and reformer and an admirer of Abraham Lincoln. At the age of fifty-six he was made Bishop of Massachusetts, but died eighteen months after his consecration in 1893.

'O Little Town of Bethlehem' was brought to Britain by W Garrett Horder, in his *Treasury of Hymns*, 1896. It has been set to two melodies, both of which I enjoy. It became a favourite of carol singers when set to Vaughan Williams' arrangement of a tune of an English folk song, 'The

Ploughboy's Dream'. As an enthusiastic collector of folk melodies, Vaughan Williams travelled the countryside, meeting the people who were still singing them. He recovered a treasure trove of songs. This one was sung to him in 1903 by Mr Garman, a farm labourer of Forest Green near Ockley in Surrey and Vaughan Williams renamed the melody the more mundane 'Forest Green' after the village. Carol singers love to sing this carol in the open air; its picture of Bethlehem under the stars could easily be transferred to imagining an English village.

Another version is by Henry Walford Davies. This marvellous tune is called 'Wengen' and is the one usually performed in the Nine Lessons and Carols at King's College Cambridge. Sir Walford Davies was an interesting character with a long and varied musical life. He was born on the English/Welsh border in Oswestry, the seventh of nine hildren of John and Sarah Whitridge Davies, and the youngest of their four surviving sons. His father was big in the local music scene and he encouraged his family to make music, so Henry and his siblings grew up playing any and every instrument they could get hold of. Henry's talents as a singer were recognised and, with some discomfort to his Nonconformist family, he became a chorister at St George's, Windsor. So at the age of twelve he was singing a gruelling fourteen services a week – as well as going to school of course. Walford Davies (his middle name Walford was his grandmother's maiden name) was also a talented organist and held the position of organist of the Temple Church in London for twenty years. He succeeded Sir Edward Elgar as Master of the King's Music, remaining in the job until 1941. His choral arrangement of another carol, 'The Holly and the Ivy', became famous through its broadcast performances in the King's College carol services.

Walford Davies was a great proponent of making classical music accessible to the masses and he found his ideal platform during the 1920s and 30s with his popular BBC series called 'Music and the Ordinary Listener'. He died in 1941 in Bristol, and is buried in the cathedral grounds there.

I've been associated with this carol since I was at Bangor Cathedral.

It explores deep meaning yet it also shows its origins as a work written for children – as many carols were. There's an internal rhyme in each verse that recreates a lovely chiming almost nursery-rhyme quality, as in the first: 'Above thy *deep* and dreamless *sleep*' and then 'The hopes and *fears* of all the *years*.' It's full of contrast as far as dynamic is concerned. The first verse is silent, otherworldly. The reality comes to you in the third verse, again, when I'm involved in it, performed very quietly, in a still fashion. The last verse can be organs blazing with a descant. It's all about casting sin out and living as pure a life as you possibly can. But even in a world of sin, as long as you've an open heart, Christ will enter.

You also have to have quite good breath to sing this carol. There are lots of lines that go over into other lines. For instance in the first verse:

> Above thy deep and dreamless sleep
> The silent stars go by.
> Yet in thy dark streets shineth
> The everlasting light,
> The hopes and fears of all the years
> Are met in thee tonight.

Every two lines are basically one line, and it's the same all the way through.

My favourite lines towards the end of verse three are 'Where meek souls will receive him, *still*/the dear Christ enters in'; the meaning slipping from one line to another with a simple stress that speaks volumes.

I've had the pleasure of performing 'O Little Town of Bethlehem' on two occasions in Israel, once as a boy, and then I got to perform it in Bethlehem for the television programmes I was producing for the BBC and recently for my programme for ITV discovering the stories behind the carols.

The Bethlehem I experienced as a man was very, very different to the Bethlehem I was introduced to as a boy. The place has changed beyond all recognition. There was more of an innocence in the Bethlehem of old, whereas today it's a bustling, busy place, which made the carol even more poignant. I was filmed in the centre of the town, with cars going past, horns hooting, people shouting. And there am I in the middle miming 'Oh little town of Bethlehem/How still we see thee lie.' Ironic, really.

But there's something magical about singing 'O Little Town of Bethlehem' in Bethlehem itself. As a child in the school congregation or if you're lucky enough to sing in a choir, you have no idea really what Bethlehem would be like. As a child I had my own preconceived idea and I remember saying to my mum and dad that I could not quite believe the fact that I actually was in Bethlehem, singing a carol about Jesus' Nativity in the place where he was born. It was a surreal – and life-changing – experience.

18

JOY TO THE WORLD

WORDS
Isaac Watts (1674–1748)

MUSIC
'Antioch' Lowell Mason (1792–1872)

Joy to the world! the Lord is come:
Let earth receive her King!
Let ev'ry heart prepare him room,
And heav'n and nature sing!

Joy to the earth! the Saviour reigns:
Let men their songs employ,
While fields and floods, rocks, hills, and plains,
Repeat the sounding joy.

93

No more let sins and sorrows grow,
Nor thorns infest the ground;
He comes to make his blessings flow
Far as the curse is found.

He rules the world with truth and grace,
And makes the nations prove
The glories of his righteousness,
And wonders of his love.

In Isaac Watts' book with the breathtaking title: *Logic, or The Right Use of Reason in the Enquiry After Truth With a Variety of Rules to Guard Against Error in the Affairs of Religion and Human Life*, as well as in the *Sciences* – phew! – he defines judgement as '. . . when mere ideas are joined in the mind without words . . .' while a proposition is when those ideas are ' . . . clothed with words . . .'

So one of Watts' best-known works 'Joy to the World' is by nature more of a proposition than a judgement. Nevertheless, before some gentle judgement is made of a carol that celebrates Christ's Second Coming, it must first be said that it provokes strong emotion, is a joy to sing, and whenever I've sung it as a member of the congregation of *Songs of Praise*, it really does what it says on the tin and makes the whole place come alive.

Isaac Watts is dubbed the 'father of English hymnody' and the 'poet of the sanctuary'. He was not an imposing figure, described two hundred years after his birth as 'Scarcely more than five feet in stature, his bodily presence was weak, his forehead was low, his cheek-bones rather prominent, his eyes small and gray, and his face in repose, of a heavy aspect.' But his precise and clear voice commanded attention and his words and singing voice captured the soul. He was named after his father Isaac, and like his father, who was imprisoned a couple of times for his dissenting convictions, Watts was a Nonconformist. Practically, this meant that he was educated at a free grammar school in Stoke Newington and was not permitted to go to either Oxford or Cambridge.

Watts was let down by his poor health for much of his life. His pastorate in London involved preaching and training future preachers, but when illness led him to cut down on his pastoral duties, Sir Thomas Abney MP, a former Lord Mayor of the City of London, invited Watts to live on his estate in Hertfordshire and in his property in Stoke Newington. There he stayed for most of the time until his death in Stoke Newington in 1748. On the anniversary of his arrival, Watts dropped a note to Abney's widow Mary saying that, having intended to stay one night '. . . I have extended my visit to the length of exactly thirty years . . .'

Free of a level of responsibility and public work, Watts' health improved. In 1719 he produced another publication with a long title, *The Psalms of David: Imitated in the Language of the New Testament, and Applied to the Christian State and Worship*. Here he paraphrases the psalms to suit a Christian audience. The source of Watts' lyrics for 'Joy to the World' is Psalm 98, which tells us to glorify Christ's triumphant Second Coming:

> Let the sea roar, and the fullness thereof; the world and they
> that dwell therein.
> Let the floods clap their hands: let the hills be joyful together
> Before the Lord, for he cometh to judge the earth:
> With righteousness shall he judge the world, and the people
> with equity.

Many of the carols I've chosen for this book tell the story of Christ as a child born to Mary in a humble stable. This one is different. The original doesn't refer specifically to Christmas and it can be sung at many times of the year, but its heading reads 'The Messiah's Coming and Kingdom' and it has become a firm favourite for Christmas.

Watts wrote over 750 hymns, many of them still familiar, including 'When I Survey the Wondrous Cross' or 'Come Let Us Join Our Cheerful Songs'. His poetry is not so well known today; one of his poems for the edification of children, 'Against Idleness and Mischief', was shamelessly used by Lewis Carroll in *Alice's Adventures in Wonderland*, becoming 'How Doth the Little Crocodile'. Maybe in revenge for Watts 'Against Idleness . . .', a playground parody of 'Joy to the World', popular with American kids, goes with homicidal intent:

> Joy to the world our teacher's dead,
> We barbecued the head . . .

Altogether, Watts' compositions have a straightforward and simple power. He had a natural gift for language and could break down the distance between the singer and the words to create an authentic connection to God and invest the song with personal meaning. He introduced the idea of using poetry that did not come directly from the Bible, but from the worshippers' own experience, which is perhaps a key to the popularity of his verses.

In 1839, Lowell Mason, who wrote over 1,600 hymn tunes and, as choir director and organist, initiated in his church the first Sunday School for Black children in America, wrote the music of 'Antioch' to go with Watts' lyrics. After some difficulties, in 1822 Mason at last found a publisher for the collection of his tunes that, following the British model, took their influence from classical European composers such as Mozart and Haydn. This was published anonymously because Mason was concerned that giving his name would jeopardise his career as a banker!

Mason was much criticised in his native North America for his leanings towards European musical tradition, and his pieces did tend to overwhelm home-grown compositions that were part of a more participatory American tradition. 'Joy to the World' was caught up in this debate; some have found the tune indistinguishable from a melody by George Frideric Handel (1685–1759), raising doubts that it is actually composed by Mason. It has been noted that the tune for the refrain 'And heaven and nature sing' features in the opening statement and accompaniment to 'Comfort Ye' in Handel's *Messiah*, and the first four words echo 'Lift up your heads' from the same oratorio.

Watts' version is not the only one of 'Joy to the World' sung today. William Wines Phelps (1792–1872) an early leader of the Latter Day Saints Movement, better known as the Mormon Church, adapted Watts' 'Joy to the World' with subtle changes around the concept of anticipating the arrival of Christ as opposed to celebrating his actual second coming.

But Watts' rendering continues to be the most popular. There are also other arrangements to add to Mason's, but one very popular one is John Rutter's; he recorded a version in the style of Handel with the Cambridge Singers for their Christmas albums in 1983 (*Christmas Star*) and 1989 (*Christmas with the Cambridge Singers*).

Over the years, this exultant piece has been recorded by many choirs. It has also been on albums by popular artists such as Andy Williams and Boney M. Mariah Carey's rendition included the opening refrain of the version written by folk singer Hoyt Axton which was a number one hit for Three Dog Night in 1971: 'Jeremiah was a bullfrog/Was a good friend of mine.' This has little resemblance to Watts' lyrics or Mason's music beyond the title but like the original it does call upon the audience to take part in its rousing rendition. And I have to include my favourite: punk rock band The Vandals named their 1996 collection of Christmas-themed songs *Oi to the World*.

It is easy to apply the judgement – or is it the proposition, as defined by Watts? – that his carol is truly inspirational.

19

LITTLE DONKEY

WORDS AND MUSIC
Eric Boswell (1921–2009)

Little donkey, little donkey
On a dusty road
Got to keep on plodding onwards
With your precious load.

Been a long time little donkey
Through the winter's night.
Don't give up now little donkey,
Bethlehem's in sight.

Ring out those bells tonight
Bethlehem, Bethlehem.
Follow the star tonight
Bethlehem, Bethlehem.

Little donkey, little donkey
Had a heavy day,
Little donkey carry Mary
Safely on her way.

Little donkey, little donkey
Journey's end is near
There are wise men waiting
For a sign to bring them here.

Do not falter, little donkey
There's a star ahead
It will guide you, little donkey
To a cattle shed.

Ring out those bells tonight
Bethlehem, Bethlehem.
Follow the star tonight
Bethlehem, Bethlehem.

Little donkey, little donkey
Had a heavy day
Little donkey carry Mary
Safely on her way,
Little donkey carry Mary
Safely on her way.

LITTLE DONKEY

This is a carol I first got to hear in Llandegfan Primary School, although I never played Joseph, Mary or the donkey for that matter. But picture the scene: I was one of the wise men with a tea towel over the head and a belt holding the thing in place.

'Little Donkey' is the sort of carol you only have to hear a few times and it soaks up into your soul; it's very easy to remember, so much so that it's probably one of the favourite carols of my daughter and now my son who's five because it's so accessible to them. And the whole idea of this tired donkey needing our support to get to its destination is a lovely one really. It's also a carol that sets the scene absolutely beautifully for a child. It's saying to this weary little donkey moving slowly through the winter's night not to give up, not to give up, Bethlehem's in sight. 'If you don't believe me there are wise men waiting to help you, there's also a star to guide you, those bells in Bethlehem are ringing out and Mary your precious cargo couldn't get there without you.' The image of Joseph with Mary on a donkey is eloquent, reinterpreted countless times on our Christmas cards and sung in school carol concerts.

The Christmas story has been enriched through its history by many such details and this one is rooted in the Gospel of Luke. Luke tells us that the Roman Emperor Augustus (27BC – AD14) on a tax-collecting spree, ordered a census to be taken of the Roman world. Joseph's ancestral home was Bethlehem, and to be counted, he and Mary had to leave Nazareth and travel more than seventy miles to Bethlehem to register there. It's not actually recorded how they travelled to Bethlehem, but riding a donkey was the most common kind of transport for poor people. It would have been a long, arduous and perhaps frightening journey, especially for Mary who was heavily pregnant, but we can only imagine her feelings about it all as they're not described in the Gospel or in this carol.

'Little Donkey' is a twentieth-century Christmas song. Eric Boswell, who wrote the words and the music in the 1950s, was a Geordie, born in the Millfield district of Sunderland on 18 July 1921, the son of a tailor and a housewife. He started to learn music when he was seven and later studied under Clifford Hartley, a local organist and choirmaster. He trained as a physicist and was employed by Marconi Electronics during the Second World War. He began writing songs during this time and was inspired to write 'Little Donkey' because he wanted to provide a simple song for children to sing: 'I racked my brains to think of aspects of the Christmas story that hadn't been sung about and came up with the idea of the donkey riding into Bethlehem.' The story goes that when he took it to his music publishers he bumped into Gracie Fields, who not only liked it, but said there and then that she wanted to record it. Our Gracie, who was then sixty-one, found Boswell's complex original tune difficult to sing, so he simplified the song for her, which was the right thing to do because it became a top twenty Christmas hit for her in 1959 and the year following reached number three in a version by Nina and Frederik. Among many other cover versions, the Beverley Sisters, Vera Lynn and the George Mitchell Minstrels have recorded 'Little

Donkey'. It's also on Dame Vera Lynn's current Christmas album and was even performed at the *Songs of Praise* Big Sing in 2008. It took its place alongside two standards, 'Ding Dong Merrily on High' and 'Hark ! The Herald Angels Sing'.

Eric Boswell apparently had mixed feelings about 'Little Donkey'. Although delighted that he had composed such a popular carol he felt that it perhaps overshadowed his other achievements. He was a songwriter, who had written 'I'll Know Her' for Matt Munro, and was well known in the north-east of England for his funny songs in the Geordie dialect such as 'I've Got a Little Whippet' and 'The Social Security Waltz'. But 'Little Donkey' was such a commercial success (it's even available as a ringtone) that Boswell never had to worry about money. It's tempting to imagine that his story was behind the plot of the film of Nick Hornby's *About a Boy* (2002), where Will Freeman played by Hugh Grant is able to have a leisurely, work-free lifestyle because his father had earned a fortune in royalties by writing a Christmas song that was played annually in supermarkets across the land.

Eric Boswell died just before Christmas in 2009, aged eighty-eight.

I can't think of this carol without seeing the school assemblies with hundreds of children sitting cross-legged giving a plodding performance of this quite plodding carol. I absolutely love it: love the melody, love the words and that it takes the child to remind the little donkey: 'you're nearly there'. It's very positive. I also have great affection for the chorus:

> Ring out those bells tonight
> Bethlehem, Bethlehem.
> Follow the star tonight
> Bethlehem, Bethlehem.

Carols like 'Away in a Manger' are also childlike in their construction and regarded by some musicologists as childish, but 'Away in a Manger' can still be performed in a performance setting whereas it's a little more difficult with 'Little Donkey' because it's now so associated with children singing it. I have recorded it myself as an adult and you do feel a little bit guilty taking away from the children a carol that so obviously belongs to them. I think in this instance the childishness is in the words, but I've been to Israel quite a few times and seen many a sad, tired-looking donkey so it may be that Eric Boswell was onto a good thing.

And such is the testimony to this carol that it can work even when it's being sung in a primary school assembly with not necessarily a music teacher, but someone with maybe only grade two or three on the piano jogging along as accompaniment. It still has a real magic and a special quality of Christmas – that is Christmas at its best as seen through a child's eyes. Perhaps the attraction to schools of 'Little Donkey' is also that it's only one octave in range for the singer and very, very easy to play. Its beauty is its simplicity. Also, what credit to this carol that people think it's a traditional folk song that has been around since the dawn of time, when actually it's a modern carol that's only been popular for the last fifty years or so.

20

THE LITTLE DRUMMER BOY

WORDS AND MUSIC
Katherine K Davis (1892–1980), Harry Simeone (1911–2005)
and Henry Onorati (?)

'Peace on Earth' words by Alan Kohan (1933–),
music by Larry Grossman (1938–) and Ian Fraser (1933–)

Come they told me pa-rum-pum-pum-pum
A new-born king to see pa-rum-pum-pum-pum
Our finest gifts we bring pa-rum-pum-pum-pum
Rum-pum-pum-pum, rum-pum-pum-pum.

Come they told me pa-rum-pum-pum-pum
A new-born king to see pa-rum-pum-pum-pum
Our finest gifts we bring pa-rum-pum-pum-pum
To lay before the king pa-rum-pum-pum-pum
Rum-pum-pum-pum, rum-pum-pum-pum
So to honour him pa-rum-pum-pum-pum
When we come.

Little baby pa-rum-pum-pum-pum
I stood beside him there pa-rum-pum-pum-pum
I played my drum for him pa-rum-pum-pum-pum
I played my best for him pa-rum-pum-pum-pum
Rum-pum-pum-pum, rum-pum-pum-pum
And he smiled at me pa-rum-pum-pum-pum
Me and my drum.

Peace on earth, can it be
Years from now, perhaps we'll see,
See the day of glory,
See the day, when men of good will
Live in peace, live in peace again.

Peace on earth, can it be
Every child must be made aware,
Every child must be made to care,
Care enough for his fellow man
To give all the love that he can.

I pray my wish will come true
For my child and your child too.
He'll see the day of glory,
See the day when men of good will
Live in peace, live in peace again.

Peace on Earth, can it be
Can it be.

The words for this song, originally 'The Carol and the Drum', came to its author in 1941 while she was trying to take a nap. Katherine K Davis (1892–1980), American composer and pianist, had the feeling that the words wrote themselves. It was not long before most music publishers started to put two other names, Henry Onorati and Harry Simeone, beside Davis in the writing credits (perhaps overstating their contributions). They each provided an arrangement of Davis' song. Onorati wrote his in 1957 for a recording which missed Christmas so was not released. The following year Simeone was asked by 20th Century Fox Records to produce a Christmas album. He formed the Harry Simeone Chorale and recorded his own arrangement under a new title, 'The Little Drummer Boy' – it was a hit. Simeone and his Chorale went on to have another with his arrangement of 'Do You Hear What I Hear' in 1962.

'The Little Drummer Boy' tells of a poor boy who can only offer the sound of his drum to the baby Jesus. Although it might be thought unwise to bang a drum up close to a newborn baby, Jesus rewards him with a smile of gratitude; the drummer boy has given Jesus his true self. To offer our skills and our abilities is worth more than to lavish expensive gifts that cost us nothing but money. The snowbound 'In the Bleak Midwinter' also celebrates humble and honest generosity as an expression of devotion in a complementary way to this modern carol.

In essence the story of the drummer boy echoes an oft-related twelfth-century tale. A juggler is reprimanded for singing vulgar songs outside a monastery. He is taken inside where he repents and joins the Order. One day he watches other monks laying rich gifts before the newly sculpted statue of the Virgin Mary. The boy is poor and has no presents to offer her. Late at night he creeps into the chapel and performs a juggling act at the foot of the pedestal. The statue comes to life and the Virgin blesses him, in some versions with a smile, in others with a rose. As Mary ascends to Heaven she beckons to the juggler to follow her. He drops dead and does as she commands. Witnessing this miracle, the monks declare him a saint.

In 1892 Anatole France published this story as '*Le Jongleur de Notre Dame*' and in 1902 Jules Massenet turned it into an opera of the same name.

Bing Crosby made his first recording of 'The Little Drummer Boy' song in 1962. Any seasonal song was safe in Crosby's hands, who had had his big Christmas hit with Irving Berlin's 'White Christmas', performed by Bing in the 1954 movie *White Christmas*. This was no exception. The recording is still available today, as it was then, on Crosby's *I Wish You A Merry Christmas* 1962 album.

Then in 1977 there was what many consider to be one of the oddest pairings in duet history. The then glam-rocker David Bowie joined up with Bing to perform 'The Little Drummer Boy' for a recording of Crosby's Christmas Special in a hot September. The makers of the Special took advantage of Crosby's tour of Britain to film the show in the UK. On his arrival at Elstree Studios, to the set of a fake medieval castle supposed to be Crosby's home during his stay in Britain, David Bowie threw the producers into confusion when he announced that he disliked the song. He did not want to sing it. Writers Ian Fraser, Larry Grossman and Alan Kohan found a piano in the studio's basement and got to work.

They wrote 'Peace on Earth' in an hour and a half.

The melody and lyrics are a counterpoint to the original song and follow after Davis' last verse. Bowie agreed to sing the new version. The two men's voices create a smooth and soulful harmony and theirs turned out to be a match made in Heaven. For some years this new song was available only as a bootleg copy. In 1982 it was released as a single and it went to number three in the UK on Christmas Day.

Six weeks after recording the song, on 14 October, Bing Crosby had a fatal heart attack on a golf course in Spain.

Other artists who have sung 'The Little Drummer Boy' include the Von Trapp family, Marlene Dietrich, Nana Mouskouri, Boney M and Whitney Houston, who sang it with her daughter Bobbi Kristina Brown.

What a year 2008 was. I'd been asked by TOGGS, Terry's Old Gals and Geezers, to do a charity single of the Bowie/Crosby arrangement with Terry Wogan taking Bing's part. I'd never recorded 'The Little Drummer Boy' as a child and, to be brutally honest, it wasn't my favourite carol. I love the message in the carol that we are at all times to be the best that we can be, and at all times to be ourselves. I think that's a fantastic message, which I've tried to be true to throughout my life. And it's not every day that you get to go into the studio with Sir Terry Wogan. That's exactly what we did. He'd finished his morning programme at 9.30. By ten o'clock we were facing one another in fits of laughter, recording this song. Miraculously and without really thinking about it, because, let's face it, Terry's far too busy to be thinking about Christmas carols, he was completely himself on this. He knows he hasn't got the

greatest voice in the world, maybe not the greatest voice in Britain, maybe not even the greatest voice in London, or in the studio that day. He delivered it as Terry Wogan would so that the innate message of the carol came through. It also shows off Terry's rich voice beautifully, the fact that he's been on the radio for so many years, the fact that his voice resonates with so many people – that vibrant, ringing tone was there in the recording of the carol. His weighty voice paired with my more lyrical, higher voice suits the song well. There's a part where we sing together and the blend is fantastic.

I've always joked, as has Terry on the radio, that he's my illegitimate radio father, therefore I am his illegitimate radio son and when we were in the studio together, it really was a feeling of father and son. He's somebody I look up to massively on the radio and it was quite nice seeing him out of his environment and actually in mine – roles were reversed somewhat; usually he's in the studio and I'm there with my tongue lolling out worshipping the ground he walks on because I think he's one of the greatest broadcasters in the world, so to see the roles reversed was quite interesting.

The highlight of the carol for me again, even going back to the recording with Sir Terry, is the counter melody I get to sing against his pa-rum-pum-pum-pums, especially because the words are really poignant for this day and age: 'Peace on earth, can it be/Years from now, perhaps we'll see/See the day of glory/See the day, when men of good will/Live in peace, live in peace again.' Then the final verse, as if both reiterating and bringing in a more religious aspect of it: 'I pray my wish will come true/For my child and your child too . . .'

So – a perfect carol for these times and little did we know that by going into the studio we'd create a single that actually got a higher ranking in the charts than a Christmas song I'm most well known for, which is 'Walking in the Air'. 'Walking in the Air' got to number five in the charts, while this got to number three, and if it weren't for being up against *The X Factor* winner Alexandra Burke, then I think we would have got to number one. (In fact, on physical sales alone we would have been number one by miles – she was ahead by 200,000 on download.) But we got to record the video in Cliveden House hotel and to my dying day I'll remember walking out of Cliveden to find that the production team had sprayed this fake snow everywhere. I looked into the Cliveden restaurant from outside and could see that there were three tables occupied by people having lunch, two American tables and I think a business couple from Britain, and their jaws were on the floor because they couldn't believe that they were actually seeing fake snow in Cliveden on a beautifully sunny day and Sir Terry Wogan and myself dressed in woollen coats, and scarves, and hats. It was a surreal scene. Needless to say we signed lots of autographs that day.

It was a wonderful experience being involved in this carol and I never realised it would be so popular until Chris Evans, who has more energy than anyone I've ever met, took it upon himself to make it Christmas number one. He would be ringing me constantly saying 'What happened today? Who've you got involved now?' So I managed to get a record company to record it and release it and then a promotions company to look after it. Every night Chris Evans would have a 'Little Drummer Boy' update and I think his audience by the end were fed up hearing it, but it was an incredible Christmas and a very, very exciting time. Wouldn't it be good if the message of this simple carol one day did come true?

21

ONCE IN ROYAL DAVID'S CITY

WORDS   MUSIC
Cecil Frances Alexander (1818–95)   Henry John Gauntlett (1805–76)

Once in Royal David's city
Stood a lowly cattle shed,
Where a mother laid her baby
In a manger for his bed.
Mary was that mother mild,
Jesus Christ her little child.

He came down to earth from heaven
Who is God and Lord of all
And his shelter was a stable
And his cradle was a stall;
With the poor and mean and lowly
Lived on earth our Saviour holy.

And through all his wondrous childhood
He would honour and obey,
Love and watch the lowly maiden
In whose gentle arms he lay.
Christian children all must be
Mild, obedient, good as he.

For he is our childhood's pattern:
Day by day like us he grew;

ONCE IN ROYAL
DAVID'S CITY

109

Once in royal David's city

C.F. Alexander

H.J. Gauntlett

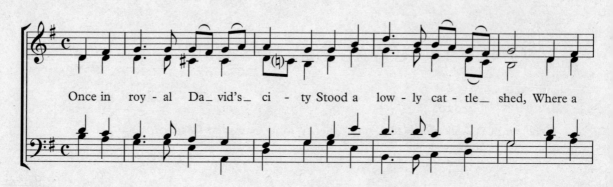

Once in roy - al Da_ vid's_ ci - ty Stood a low - ly cat - tle_ shed, Where a

moth - er laid_ her_ ba - by In a man - ger for_ His_ bed. Ma - ry

was that moth - er mild, Je - sus Christ her lit - tle_ child.

He was little, weak and helpless,
Tears and smiles like us he knew;
And he feeleth for our sadness,
And he shareth in our gladness.

And our eyes at last shall see him
Through his own redeeming love,
For that Child so dear and gentle
Is our Lord in heaven above;
And he leads his children on
To the place where he is gone.

Not in that poor lowly stable,
With the oxen standing by
We shall see him, but in heaven,
Set at God's right hand on high,
When, like stars, his children crowned
All in white shall wait around.

ONCE IN ROYAL
DAVID'S CITY

III

Probably the most famous carol in the whole book, 'Once in Royal David's City' is famous for so many reasons. Of course this is an amazing carol, a beautiful blend of music and words. But also in the way it's used these days, in Nine Lessons and Carols from King's College, Cambridge for instance, by all accounts it's become so famous that the choristers are always so nervous before performing it and of course the first verse is always sung by a boy soloist. Because of the nerve situation, he is chosen at the very last minute, usually about twenty or thirty seconds before the broadcast, so the nerves don't get the better of the poor chap. The second verse is sung by the choir, and the congregation joins in the third.

Not many people have heard of the carol's author Cecil Frances Alexander, but millions of us naturally have heard her work sung every

Christmas. Perhaps we've grown up singing her best-known poems at school assemblies and in church. Her hymns 'There is a Green Hill Far Away' and 'All Things Bright and Beautiful' have been enjoyed by generations and have caused controversy too (for the story of the debate surrounding 'All Things Bright and Beautiful' see my *Forty Favourite Hymns*).

Since Hildegarde of Bingen put pen to paper in the twelfth century, hymn writing has been considered a suitable occupation for a woman and flourished through the nineteenth century. Like her contemporaries Charlotte Elliott (1789–1871) and Christina Rossetti (1830–94), Cecil Frances Alexander wrote many hymns and poems – about 400 in her case – during the second half of Queen Victoria's reign. She was born in Dublin in 1818 and brought up in Dublin's Anglo-Irish community. Her father managed the estates of the Earl of Wicklow. Cecil Frances had quite a few suitors; her choice was the Reverend William Alexander, whom she married in 1850. William became Archbishop of Armagh and the Primate of All Ireland.

Cecil Frances Alexander was by inclination a teacher. She wrote her *Hymns for Little Children* in 1848. The book included 'Once in Royal David's City'. It became a nineteenth-century bestseller in the UK, where it went to 100 editions, and through the rest of the world. *Hymns for Little Children* was laid out in the form of the Church Catechism. Through its fourteen hymns, Cecil Frances set out to explain the sections of the Apostles' Creed. 'Once in Royal David's City' was the eleventh hymn in the Creed, coming immediately before 'There is a Green Hill Far Away', which explores what the lines 'he was crucified, dead and buried' mean. Cecil Frances made no money from this collection, as she donated her royalties towards the building and maintenance of a school for the deaf in Strabane, which she had founded.

Henry John Gauntlett, composer of the tune called 'Irby' that fits so well with Cecil Frances' verses, was a lawyer until he was forty, when he gave up the law to devote the rest of his life to music. Thenceforth, he made up for the lost time given to legal matters by writing a mind-

boggling 10,000-plus hymn tunes. When the muse was absent, he put into action his perception that the organ was an instrument with potential to be a more flexible musical device, patenting a new electrical-action apparatus for it. Gauntlett's invention combined the lightness of touch of the tubular-pneumatic action it was replacing – the means of transferring the action of the keys and the stops to the pipes – with a faster response.

Gauntlett's simple melody was first arranged not for organ but as a piano accompaniment and in 1849 it was published in a pamphlet called *Christmas Carols, Four Numbers*. It did not get the name 'Irby' until it was included in the 1861 first edition of *Hymns Ancient and Modern*. It is not clear why the tune was called this. Gauntlett doesn't appear to have had a connection with any of the places in the UK called Irby, nor with the Irby in Southern Ireland that these days is a few hours' drive from Londonderry where Cecil Frances once lived. The house today boasts a blue plaque commemorating her time there.

Cecil Frances' *Hymns for Little Children* is dedicated to her 'little Godsons'. She is supposed to have written the book in response to their complaint that learning the catechism for their confirmation was boring and difficult. She expresses the hope that the 'language of verse which children love may help to impress on their minds what they are, what I have promised them, and what they must seek to be.' This message demonstrates a Victorian idolisation of childhood, which Cecil Frances subscribed to, and of which 'Once in Royal David's City' is a good example. The human baby Jesus, who cries and smiles as they do, demonstrates to children what they can indeed 'seek to be'.

This inspirational carol still communicates a powerful message, not only to children but to all of us. 'Once in Royal David's City' celebrates the wondrous event that occurred so many centuries ago in Bethlehem; for many this carol signals the start of Christmas.

In my days as a chorister I sang 'Once in Royal David's City' as part of the choir of Bangor Cathedral and I was always bowled over by its majesty, the fact that it can start so quietly and really does build up.

These days my association with this carol is through the charity event that I take part in in Handel's church, St George's Hanover Square, where Westminster Cathedral choristers sing 'Once in Royal David's City' as we process into the church ready for our very own Nine Lessons and Carols. It's an event for which Judi Dench is the President and I'm the Vice President and lessons are read by such actors as Anthony Hopkins, Charles Dance and the like.

As a boy soprano I was very fortunate to perform 'Once in Royal David's City' in Israel in one of two programmes made there by the BBC. I was the guest soloist, so I'd recorded all the music back in Britain, and then I went over to Israel to mime these holy pieces in their environment. It was the morning that I was supposed to be driving to the Wailing Wall to perform the carol, which was being filmed by an Israeli film crew as a joint production between Israeli Television and British TV and this was going to be a special programme for Christmas Eve. We were in the back of the van and two minutes before we arrived at our destination, a huge bomb had gone off so we were sent on a detour. I remember as a boy being in the back of this van with my parents and the British producer, feeling slightly scared to say the least, knowing that I was about to perform what I regarded as an amazing Godlike carol in an area where I thought bombs and hatred didn't really exist. It shows that as a child I wasn't really aware of the dangerous and frightening situation I was in. But once I got to the Wailing Wall there was no sign of bombs or anything like that, just a friendly Israeli film crew with lots of cameras, a crowd of tourists looking on, and a little Aled Jones in grey trousers, blue shirt and a terrible blue bow tie performing 'Once in Royal David's City'. I think it was about seven o'clock in the morning as well. That's an experience that will remain with me forever.

Of the many descants that have been written for this carol, my favourite is again by a person I've been very fortunate to get to know through my life and that's Sir David Willcocks. His descant, especially on the sixth verse: 'Not in that poor lowly stable/With the oxen standing by' is so uplifting, and when you get to the two last lines: 'When, like

stars, his children crowned/All in white shall wait around' with the descant – and I'm very lucky that at Christmas we have the Band of the Irish Guards playing along – you can imagine the scene: a packed church, six hundred people, the Band of the Irish Guards, Westminster Cathedral Choir and congregation all belting out this glorious carol. Then it really does make the hairs at the back of your neck stand up.

ONCE IN ROYAL
DAVID'S CITY

22

MARY HAD A BABY

Collected by N G J Ballanta-Taylor (1893–1962)

Mary had a baby, my Lord,
Mary had a baby, oh my Lord,
Mary had a baby, my Lord,
People keep a-comin' an' the train done gone.
What did she name him? my Lord,
What did she name him? oh my Lord,
What did she name him? my Lord,
People keep a-comin' an' the train done gone.
She named him Jesus, my Lord,
She named him Jesus, oh my Lord,
She named him Jesus, my Lord,
People keep a-comin' an' the train done gone.
Named him King Jesus, my Lord,
Named him King Jesus, oh my Lord,
Named him King Jesus, my Lord,
People keep a-comin' an' the train done gone.
Now where was he born? my Lord,
Where was he born? oh my Lord,
Where was he born? my Lord,
People keep a-comin' an' the train done gone.
Born in a stable, my Lord,
Born in a stable, oh my Lord,
Born in a stable, my Lord,
People keep a-comin' an' the train done gone.

And where did she lay him? My Lord,
Where did she lay him? oh my Lord,
Where did she lay him? my Lord,
People keep a-comin' an' the train done gone.
She laid him in a manger, my Lord,
Laid him in a manger, oh my Lord,
Laid him in a manger, my Lord,
People keep a-comin' an' the train done gone.
Who heard the singing? my Lord,
Who heard the singing? oh my Lord,
Who heard the singing? my Lord,
People keep a-comin' an' the train done gone.
Shepherds heard the singing, my Lord,
Shepherds heard the singing, oh my Lord,
Shepherds heard the singing, my Lord,
People keep a-comin' an' the train done gone.
Who came to see him? my Lord,
Who came to see him? oh my Lord,
Who came to see him? my Lord,
People keep a-comin' an' the train done gone.
Shepherds came to see him, my Lord,
Shepherds came to see him, oh my Lord,
Shepherds came to see him, my Lord,
People keep a-comin' an' the train done gone.
Star keeps shining, my Lord,
Star keeps shining, oh my Lord,
Star keeps shining, my Lord,
People keep a-comin' an' the train done gone.
The wise men kneeled before him, my Lord,
The wise men kneeled before him, oh my Lord,
The wise men kneeled before him, my Lord,
People keep a-comin' an' the train done gone.
King Herod tried to find him, my Lord,

King Herod tried to find him, oh my Lord,
King Herod tried to find him, my Lord,
People keep a-comin' an' the train done gone.
Moving in the elements, my Lord,
Moving in the elements, oh my Lord,
Moving in the elements, my Lord,
People keep a-comin' an' the train done gone.
They went away to Egypt, my Lord,
They went away to Egypt, oh my Lord,
They went away to Egypt, my Lord,
People keep a-comin' an' the train done gone.
Traveled on a donkey, my Lord,
Traveled on a donkey, oh my Lord,
Traveled on a donkey, my Lord,
People keep a-comin' an' the train done gone.
Angels watching over him, my Lord,
Angels watching over him, oh, my Lord,
Angels watching over him, my Lord,
People keep a-comin' an' the train done gone.

The origins of 'Mary Had a Baby' have been traced to St Helena Island off the coast of South Carolina. It is a traditional Christmas song and is maybe more a spiritual than a carol.

Spirituals set out to communicate Christian ideals, but they also spoke of the hardship of being an African-American slave and their lyrics were often directly linked to the composer's experience. The spiritual offered slaves an expressive way of sharing their religious, emotional, and physical experiences. The passion of the music could remind its singers that Jesus was always by their side looking after them. Today, in entirely different circumstances, this sense of being connected is still evoked by spirituals.

We owe a debt to the forensic skills of the musicologist N G J Ballanta-Taylor for diligently collecting the words and music of many spirituals, among them 'Mary Had a Baby'. Ballanta-Taylor was building on the work of the abolitionists William Francis Allen (1830–89), Lucy McKim Garrison (1842–77) and Charles Pickard Ware (1849–1921). During the American Civil War of 1861 to 1865, their work with freed slaves on plantations moved the authors to transcribe the tunes and lyrics of slave songs. Published in 1867, *Slave Songs of the United States* was the first and most influential collection of African American music.

Nicholas George Julius Ballanta-Taylor, born near Freetown in Sierra Leone in 1893, was the son of Gustavus Taylor, a ship's engineer who played the violin and organ. Tragically Gustavus died in a shipping accident when his son was ten and although Nicholas was able to achieve a grammar school education in Freetown and pass the entrance exam for a music degree in England at Durham University, he could not afford to actually travel to university in the UK. However his undoubted muscial talent got him a break: he was working as musical director for the Choral Society in Freetown when he met Adelaide Casely-Hayford (1868–1960). Casely-Hayford was also born in Sierra Leone. She was an ardent feminist and advocate for preserving the national identity and cultural heritage of Sierra Leoneans. She was educated in England, to where her father had retired, and then Germany, returning to Freetown after an absence of twenty-five years. Determined to help Ballanta-Taylor's musical career, she took his choral work with her on a trip to New York and later paid for him to join her there. He was given a scholarship to the Institute of Musical Art (now the Juilliard School of Music) and met the philanthropist George Peabody who went on to fund his research into spirituals. Ballanta-Taylor's scientifically rigorous approach to this work has left a significant legacy for musicians and academics alike.

One of those musicians was William Levi Dawson.

Born in Anniston, Alabama in 1899, William Dawson ran away from home at the age of thirteen and joined the Tuskegee Institute in Alabama. This was the only school in the area that accepted African-American students. William paid for his education by working on the school's farm. He played in both the band and orchestra of Tuskegee.

Dawson received international acclaim for his most important orchestral work, *Negro Folk Symphony*. It was the first work of its nature by an African-American composer incorporating authentic African-American folk melodies in a symphonic form. The symphony was premiered by the Philadelphia Orchestra under the direction of conductor Leopold Stokowski in 1934. Life came around full circle for William when he returned to the Tuskegee Institute and was professor there. He developed the 100-member Tuskegee choir, formed by the school's founder, Booker T Washington. While he was their conductor – from 1931 to 1956 – William took the choir out on tour and they gained a worldwide reputation, singing at Carnegie Hall in New York and at the White House.

Although he is best known for his contributions to both orchestral and choral literature, perhaps Dawson's most celebrated works are his arrangements and variations of spiritual songs such as those collected by his near contemporary, Nicholas Ballanta-Taylor. Dawson's many recordings and sheet music have assured that 'Mary Had a Baby' is a well-loved favourite at the festive season. It is part of a rich tradition of Christmas spirituals that include the popular 'Go Tell It on the Mountain', sung by African-American slaves labouring in the fields of the American South. William Levi Dawson died in Montgomery, Alabama in 1990 aged ninety-one.

'Mary Had a Baby' has an upbeat rhythmic tune, which is repeated throughout the song, with a key change midway. For the first few verses it is a classic call and response song: questions are answered with a key phrase, 'People keep a-comin' an' the train done gone', chanted over and over. It's a dynamic image of the crowds flocking – but too late to see the Baby Jesus. There is hidden meaning too. Spiritual songs often contained codes that referred to the situation of the singers. 'Home' was heaven but it was also an imagined haven for slaves, a place free of literal shackles. While in this instance 'train' was the transport used by fugitives escaping to a free country – giving a poignancy to the line that's repeated throughout the many verses of this song. Such 'secret messages' were a powerful path of communication between the singers and their God.

It's a carol I've never recorded before; I don't think it's a song that can only be sung by African-Americans, I think it's a song that's open to anyone. I used to sing it as a boy in school. We never sang all the twenty verses, otherwise our school assemblies would have gone on forever! It's a song that truthfully conveys the gospel arising from the good news that in Bethlehem on that special day Mary. Had. A. Baby – and that baby changed the course of the world forever.

MARY HAD
A BABY

23

MARY'S BOY CHILD

WORDS AND MUSIC
Jester Joseph Hairston (1901–2000)

Long time ago in Bethlehem,
So the Holy Bible say
Mary's boy child, Jesus Christ
Was born on Christmas day.

Hark, now hear the angels sing,
A new King born today
And man will live for evermore
Because of Christmas day.

While shepherds watched their flock by night
Them see a bright new shining star,
Them hear a choir of angels sing,
The music seems to come from afar.

Chorus

Now, Joseph and his wife Mary
Come to Bethlehem that night,
Them find no place for to born the child,
Not a single room was in sight.

Chorus

By and by they find a little nook
In a stable all forlorn,
And in a manger cold and dark
Mary's little boy was born.

Chorus

The three wise men tell old King Herod
We hear a new King born today,
We bring he frankincense and myrrh,
We come from far, far away.

Chorus

When old King Herod he learned this news,
Him mad as him can be,
He tell de wise men find this child,
So that I may worship he!

Chorus

I remember hearing 'Mary's Boy Child' for the first time on my parents' old record player. They'd gone out and bought an album by Boney M and I remembering them playing 'Mary's Boy Child' in our little house in Llandegfan – it was just before Christmas – and it having a tremendous effect on me: the harmonies, the melody line. It was unlike anything I'd heard before and this was from a boy who went to Sunday School and sang his carols and his hymns with gusto every week. But this was something different with a totally different heart and beat to it. And I loved the idea of the chorus that man will live for ever more because of Christmas because as far as I was concerned Chrismas Day was the best day of the year anyway and not just because of the birth of

Jesus but (I'm being honest now) I'd get a new bike, say, and Father Christmas would come, but also that because of Christmas Day we'd live forever, what a great thought. I must have been only about seven or eight when I first heard 'Mary's Boy Child' on that Boney M recording. The story is a lot more real and the verses tell the story in a more modern way than some of the ones I used to hear and sing in Sunday School.

Jester Joseph Hairston was not a household name when he died aged ninety-nine, just eighteen days into the twenty-first century, but he had written a song nearly fifty years earlier that still trips off our tongues. 'Mary's Boy Child' is now played in many public places at Christmas, from community halls to supermarkets. Hairston wrote the piece in 1956. It was recorded that same year by Mahalia Jackson (1911–72), the first gospel singer to perform at Carnegie Hall in New York, whose version was slightly differently titled: 'Mary's Little Boy Child'. Singer and actor Harry Connick Jr (1967–) has also recorded the song under this title.

The following year, in 1957, Harry Belafonte (1927–) included the track on his album *An Evening with Harry Belafonte*, in which he interprets folk music from around the world with songs including 'Danny Boy' and 'When the Saints Go Marching In'. Harry Belafonte became the first black singer to reach number one with 'Mary's Boy Child'. This version was also the first British number one to last longer than four minutes (by 12 seconds) and the first UK single to sell more than a million copies. Purely seasonal however, it stayed at number one for seven weeks then plummeted straight out of the top ten, becoming the first single to leave as swiftly as it had arrived.

Jester Joseph Hairston was the grandson of slaves. He was born in Belews Creek, North Carolina, grew up in Pennsylvania – where generations of his family had worked in the steel mills – and went on to study music at Tufts University and the Juilliard School in New York. In 1937 he became a founding member of the Screen Actors' Guild. He was one of the great choral directors, who found his way onto Broadway and into Hollywood as the conductor of choirs, organising the first integrated choir there, and he had a long movie and TV acting career. One can imagine what his first bit parts in the early *Tarzan* movies were

like, but talking later in his life about those roles he said, 'We had a hard time then fighting for dignity. We had no power, we had to take it, and because we took it the young people today have opportunities.' His later movie career was celebrated, from *To Kill a Mockingbird* in 1962, through to *Being John Malkovich* in 1999, just a few months before his death; he certainly earned his star on the Hollywood Walk of Fame.

As composer and arranger, Hairston dedicated himself to preserving the old Negro spirituals and 'Mary's Boy Child' is written in spiritual style. Mary, the mother of Jesus, is remarkably absent from the Christmas carols of our European traditions, coming after the shepherds and angels, and just above the wise men. She is a quiet absent presence nevertheless. Her thoughtful silence surrounded by massed angels and worshipping kings and shepherds is noted briefly and movingly by St Luke: 'But Mary kept all these things, and pondered them in her heart.' But the carol as a musical genre is rich and diverse enough to include everyone involved in the story of the Nativity and Mary takes centre stage as the subject of Christmas spirituals, including, in this book, 'Mary Had a Baby' from St Helena, or 'Mary, Don't You Weep', or 'Mary, Mary, Where is Your Baby?', which Jester Hairston also arranged.

The London Adventist Chorale under its Principal Conductor Ken Burton has performed 'Mary's Boy Child' on *Songs of Praise* with full orchestra. It was also a great pleasure for me to invite them to record this carol on my Christmas carols programme for ITV, produced at St Bartholomew's Church. I asked Ken Burton for his and the Chorale's experience of performing the carol and what it means to him:

"'Mary's Boy Child'", Ken Burton says,

is a fantastic musical celebration of the Christmas story and very satisfying to sing, thanks to its well-crafted melody. I particularly enjoy the syncopated rhythms and the angular contour of the verse's tune, which contrasts with the hymn-like majestic chorus, a truly powerful moment in the song. Any singer will relate to that wonderful feeling of release when singing a phrase such as that which opens the refrain of this carol, when the abdominal muscles combine with the most open of vowel sounds to give that brilliant burst of musical energy on the word 'Hark'. What also makes this a significant moment in the song is its connection with the words; the lighter rhythms of the verse characterise the simple telling of the Nativity story using a simple narrative language, whilst the chorus conveys the majesty of Christ. And being of the Adventist faith, the last line 'man shall live for evermore' resonates strongly with my personal belief in the hope of eternal life.

I have known this song practically all my life, and have memories of listening to many recordings of it and getting a warm feeling. It was not always appreciated by many whom I knew felt it was denigrating to refer to the Son of God as 'boy child', which is a colloquial term in many Caribbean islands. Others were uncomfortable about the phrase 'born on Christmas Day'; so whilst I listened to and enjoyed recordings of it, 'Mary's Boy Child' was not typically on the repertoire list, although I personally appreciated the poetry.

The choir (and conductor) recalls the wonderful setting and the amazing buzz in filming for the Aled Jones Christmas carols programme a song that combines the signature warm 'chestnuts roasting on an open fire' type rich-harmony choral singing, with gentle calypso rhythms, classical-style writing, and cascading lines representing myriads of angels joining in the song of praise. The atmosphere allowed the singers to appreciate the song musically and spiritually.

From early childhood memories to when I am old and grey, the song will continue to inspire me.

I agree. I think 'Mary's Boy Child' has stood the test of time: it's a heartfelt and moving song with a catchy tune that lends itself to different rhythms. Its rousing qualities can arouse strong emotions in singers and audience, its roots are deep inside popular music, and it had a real impact on a small boy in Llandegfan.

24

SEE AMID THE WINTER'S SNOW

WORDS
Edward Caswall (1814–78)

MUSIC
Sir John Goss (1800–80)

See amid the winter's snow,
Born for us on earth below,
See the tender Lamb appears,
Promised from eternal years.

Hail! Thou ever blessed morn!
Hail, redemption's happy dawn!
Sing through all Jerusalem,
Christ is born in Bethlehem.

Lo, within a manger lies
He who built the starry skies;
He who, throned in height sublime,
Sits amid the cherubim.

Chorus

Say, ye holy shepherds, say
What your joyful news today;
Wherefore have ye left your sheep
On the lonely mountain steep?

Chorus

'As we watched at dead of night,
Lo, we saw a wondrous light;
Angels singing "Peace on earth"
Told us of the Saviour's birth.'

Chorus

Sacred infant, all divine,
What a tender love was thine;
Thus to come from highest bliss
Down to such a world as this.

Chorus

Teach, O teach us, Holy Child,
By Thy face so meek and mild,
Teach us to resemble Thee,
In Thy sweet humility!

Chorus

Unlike the short simplicity of 'Away in a Manger' or the 'Coventry' and 'Rocking' carols, this carol is a generous six verses, divided by a rousing chorus. It brings to us the astonishing paradox that the baby sleeping in straw in a stable is the God 'who built the starry skies' themselves. It also stirs the imagination with its images. Like 'In the Bleak Midwinter' or 'Still, Still, Still' it pictures a cold, white Nativity. The snowy place conjured into our imaginations here seems a little strange for Bethlehem town, but the whiteness of snow is a simple way of giving the message of purity covering the sins of the world and, in the northern hemisphere at least, reflects the time we celebrate Christmas.

The shepherds are here again; this time they are asked a quite challenging question: someone, perhaps, as Luke's Gospel says, encountering the shepherds returning from the Nativity, 'glorifying and praising God', asks them why they have left their sheep alone 'On the lonely mountain steep?' They reply 'As we watched at dead of night/Lo, we saw a wondrous light.'

Edward Caswall wrote the words for 'See Amid the Winter's Snow'. He was a well-respected translator of hymns, including the hymn for Advent, 'Hark! A Herald Voice is Calling'. He was born in Yateley in Hampshire. His father the Reverend R C Caswall was vicar there and Edward too was ordained as an Anglican clergyman. But he left his living in 1846 to follow John Henry Newman (1801–90), the major figure of the Oxford Movement, into Roman Catholicism. Caswall did not become a priest but joined the Oratory of Saint Philip Neri, a community committed to being independent and self-governing without taking formal vows.

In 1871, Sir John Goss, perhaps better known for his tune 'Lauda Anima' for the hymn 'Praise my Soul, the King of Heaven', put Caswall's words to music. He was born two days after Christmas Day in 1800 as the first year of the new century drew to a close. He was in his seventies when he composed the nicely named tune 'Humility' for the carol. In the same year, 'See Amid the Winter's Snow' was guaranteed a national audience. Henry Ramsden Bramley and John Stainer selected it as a new carol for the second of their series of enormously influential collections, *Christmas Carols New and Old*. They had, as they assured readers, 'made every effort to preserve those compositions which proved their hold upon the popular mind, by their continued use up to the present time'. Goss's advice in the score is that 'See Amid the Winter's Snow' be sung as a solo by 'Treble or Tenor, or alternately'. In the collection, the carol's words are set below an engraving by Edward Dalziel (1817–1905) of snow-free rolling downland, dotted with grazing animals. This is one of many such featured in the collection by the Dalziel Brothers, a renowned family of engravers whose company provided illustrations to the work of the likes of Charles Dickens, Lewis Carroll and Edward Lear during the late nineteenth century.

Henry Ramsden Bramley and John Stainer assert that their selection for inclusion in *Christmas Carols New and Old* is designed to cater for two kinds of worshipper:

> Such carols may afford pleasure to some who are unable to make use of the more difficult productions of modern composers, while those who prefer the latter may perhaps find in the whole collection an adequate supply of words and music adapted to a more fastidious taste.

It's not clear into which of these categories they place 'See Amid the Winter's Snow'. What we do know is that it still captures minds and hearts: it came in at number twelve in the 2005 *Songs of Praise* poll.

In 1920, Caswall's hymn was published in *The St. Gregory Hymnal and Catholic Choir Book* with Goss's name replaced by the credit 'Traditional Melody'. Its editor, the conductor, composer and arranger Nicola A Montani (1880–1948) was a Knight Commander of the Order of St Sylvester, one of the five Catholic orders awarded directly by the Pope. He was also founder of the St Gregory Guild, an organisation devoted to the music of the Roman Catholic church. Montani's arrangement of the carol leaves out Caswall's two shepherds' verses.

Instead he focuses on the devotional aspect of the carol and ends with a verse of his own:

> Virgin Mother, Mary blest,
> By the joys that fill thy breast,
> Pray for us, that we may prove
> Worthy of the Saviour's love.

Thankfully, the shepherds are back in the joyous carol we sing today, putting us singers in touch with our faith.

It's a carol in the same bracket as the Big Five, the ones that you sing out with relish. 'O Come All Ye Faithful', 'Hark! The Herald Angels Sing',

'The First Nowell' . . . It's very simple in its construction, which means everyone can have a go at it, the verses are uncomplicated in their melodic structure and then it comes to the chorus, which is repetitive, monotonous, but again in a good way – it reinforces everything that's fine about this carol, in almost the same vein as our most popular hymns; the chorus is good too in that monotony adds to the message getting drummed home. I must have sung it in Bangor Cathedral. It's not one I've recorded before but I would like to have a go at it as a solo soon. I've definitely sung this carol as part of a *Songs of Praise* congregation and when you are part of the congregation it really does take a lot out of you, it requires 100 per cent commitment.

It's quite modern in its construction, especially the final verse:

> Sacred infant, all divine,
> What a tender love was thine:
> Thus to come from highest bliss
> Down to such a world as this.

It's saying that something as wonderful as Jesus could actually come down to the world he created, so it's a mixture of ancient and modern in a way.

Rocking

translated by
P. Dearmer

Traditional Czech

Lit - tle Je - sus, sweet - ly___ sleep, do not___ stir;

We will___ lend a___ coat of___ fur: We will rock you,

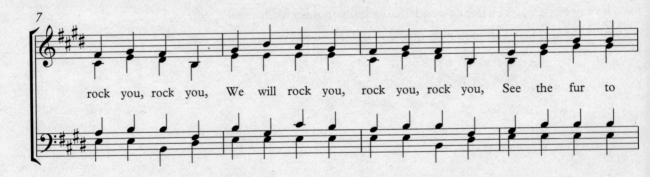

rock you, rock you, We will rock you, rock you, rock you, See the fur to

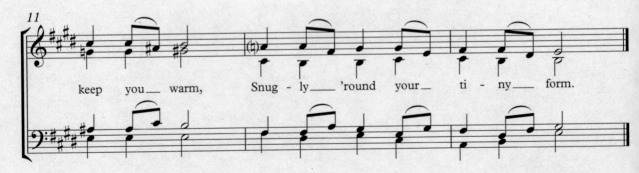

keep you___ warm, Snug - ly___ 'round your___ ti - ny___ form.

25

ROCKING CAROL

Traditional Czech lullaby

TRANSLATION   ARRANGEMENT

Percy Dearmer (1867–1936)   John Rutter (1945–)

Little Jesus, sweetly sleep, do not stir;
We will lend a coat of fur:
We will rock you, rock you, rock you,
We will rock you, rock you, rock you,
See the fur to keep you warm,
Snugly round your tiny form.

Mary's little baby, sleep, sweetly sleep,
Sleep in comfort, slumber deep;
We will rock you, rock you, rock you,
We will rock you, rock you, rock you:
We will serve you all we can,
Darling, darling little man.

I always associate 'Rocking Carol' a little bit with 'The Coventry Carol'. It's another that really does stay in your mind and your heart. Its stillness is its great quality. This is a carol that could make you go to sleep in the middle of a performance, not in a negative way but because of its beauty. And like other good lullabies, 'Rocking' is really quite sustained – the motion of 'Rock you, rock you, rock you' gives the carol its magical, rhythmic quality.

Christmas carols in the manner of lullabies are found in many cultures, from Austria with 'Still, Still, Still' and 'Silent Night' to the Cossack lullaby *Spi mladenets, moy prekrasnuy* ('Sleep baby, my dear one'), and back via England's 'Twinkle Twinkle Little Star' to this lovely Christmas lullaby from Czechoslovakia. It's very old, coming from the late Middle Ages, but it works for any age, its melody and words mimicking the soothing movement of the cradle. It's likely that 'Rocking' originally accompanied the custom of cradle rocking in German churches that spread from there across the Low Countries during the Middle Ages. The cradle stood before the altar, with a brightly coloured Christ Child visible within, and the priest would rock it enthusiastically to the rhythm of the triple-time music of a cradle song.

This lullaby carol was collected in the early 1920s by a Miss Jacubickova as '*Hajej, nynjej*' and translated freely by the master champion of carols Percy Dearmer, for his *Oxford Book of Carols* of 1928. Dearmer and this book saved many neglected English carols for Christmas and other festivals, and brought them together with more recent items. 'Carols,' Dearmer writes in his preface to the book, 'are songs with a religious impulse that are simple, hilarious, popular and modern'. They were always modern:

> The charm of an old carol lies precisely in its having been true
> to the period in which it was written, and those which are alive
> to-day retain their vitality because of this sincerity . . . A genuine
> carol may have faults of grammar, logic, and prosody; but one
> fault it never has – that of sham antiquity.

He is true to his principles in his version of this lullaby, though his final line, 'Darling, darling little man' has not caught on with everyone, and some have changed it, to for instance 'Son of God and Son of Man'. But I take great pleasure in what Percy Dearmer has done with the words

because of their steady rhythm and because of the space he allows: he's using very simple words.

'Rocking' has been arranged by John Rutter, who, like Percy Dearmer, is a lover of Christmas carols – so much so that he's become known as the musical equivalent of Dickens, synonymous with the season. He doesn't mind. 'I've a special place in my heart for its music. It's the first music I remember actually enjoying when I was a kid, and as a member of my school chapel choir the carol service was the high point of the singing year.' Choral conductor, arranger, composer, he wrote his first carol 'The Shepherd's Pipe' when he was eighteen, followed by others including 'The Star', 'Nativity' and 'Donkey' carols. Percy Dearmer would have agreed with Rutter's view that 'they have the most variegated history, from those that go back centuries to those like "Silent Night", which only really became popular when Bing Crosby sang it in *Going My Way* in 1944'. With its ancient origins, 'Rocking' has similarly had the good fortune to be taken up by Julie Andrews in the 1960s. Rutter believes carols are a form of miniature, and 'Rocking Carol' has that quality as well as demonstrating – as both Percy Dearmer and John Rutter believe – that good carols have a way of spanning the years, enjoyed by ancient and modern worshippers.

You can really put your own stamp on a carol like this. I recorded it as an adult, much to the amusement of my producers and also quite a few colleagues who work in the music industry, who were saying it's too simplistic, too boring. I think far from it; it's totally the opposite. You can put your whole heart and soul into every single word in this carol. In the second verse, 'Mary's little baby, sleep, sweetly sleep/Sleep in comfort, slumber deep', you've got three sleeps in the space of two lines and your artistry is to make all those sleeps different and to envelop the listener in your voice, make it sound so safe, so snug. The words are saying, 'See the fur to keep you warm', so it's vocal fur if you like, it's the talent to be able to make the listener or the person watching you perform a carol feel totally at ease, wrapped up in this great feeling of Christmas.

I recorded the 'Rocking Carol' as a boy on my 1985 Christmas album and want to record it again. It's definitely a carol that makes you forget all the woes and the troubles that you have in the world in those three very special minutes. It's comforting to sing and also comforting to listen to.

26

STILL, STILL, STILL

WORDS
Aled Jones

MUSIC
Anon.

Still, still, still,
Let all the earth be still,
For Mary in her arms enfolding
Hope of all the world is holding.

Sing, sing, sing,
Sweet angel voices sing,
While Jesus lies in manger dreaming,
Seraph choirs from Heaven are streaming.

Light, light, light,
The sky is filled with light,
The holy star its news a-blazing,
Sign of hope for nations raising.

STILL, STILL, STILL

137

This haunting lullaby from Salzburg in Austria does what it says on the tin; it's very tranquil, poised – everything about this carol just oozes class. And it makes people listen, listen to the message within the words but also the melody is beautiful. Its music was written in 1819, three years after 'Silent Night', another traditional carol from the city where Mozart was born. Beyond these facts, nothing is known of the composer of this carol, which describes that sense of antici-pation on the eve of Christ's birth.

The snow-bound setting of 'Still, Still, Still' is a familiar one to carol singers; this one cleverly uses the falling snow to express total silence heralding the birth of the Christ Child – and for the child who is being rocked to sleep to this carol. Snow is silent, yet so hushed and peaceful is the 'eve of our Saviour's birth' that the gently falling snowflakes can be heard.

There are different versions of 'Still, Still, Still'. Some have two verses, others four. Here is the first verse in German:

> Still, still, still,
> *Weil's Kindlein schlafen will!*
> *Maria tut es niedersingen*
> *Ihre keusche Brust darbringen,*
> Still, still, still,
> *Weil Kindlein schlafen will.*

In 1918, ninety-nine years after this carol was composed, the Wartburg Publishing House in Chicago published the *Wartburg Hymnal for Church, School and Home* edited by the splendidly named Oswald Guido Hardwig. We can find in its Christmas section at number 116 a carol with the first line: 'Hush, Hush, Hush'. In the metrical index this carol is referred to as 'Still, Still, Still' and has been translated by Frederik William Herz-berger (1859 –1930). The lyrics are very different to those of 'Still, Still, Still', although it too is about the great event that is to come and is sung to the same melody; this is how it begins:

> Hush, hush, hush!
> Behold the wondrous light!
> Who will appear? The Christ-child dear,
> For this, you know, is Holy night.
> For this, you know, is Holy night.

The publishing company that produced this hymnal was presumably named after Wartburg Castle in Germany. In this castle from May 1521 to March 1522, the German priest and philosopher Martin Luther (wrongly credited with writing 'Away in a Manger') took refuge at the request of Frederick the Wise after being excommunicated by Pope Leo X for his refusal to recant at the Diet of Worms. (This was the name of the general assembly taking place at Worms, a town on the Rhine River.) It was during this period that Martin Luther, using the name of Junker Jörg (the Knight George), was translating the New Testament into German: the first translation into a modern language for over a millennium.

'Still, Still, Still' has been recorded by a number of artists including Mannheim Steamroller, the American group that fuses classical and popular techniques and has made worldwide sales with its Christmas albums. 'Still, Still, Still' was featured on their 1988 album: *A Fresh Aire Christmas*. Other artists who have recorded this include Charlotte Church, who sings it to an original arrangement by the composer Michelle Hynson. The folk and country artist Mary Chapin Carpenter recorded it on her 2008 *Come Darkness, Come Light* album.

I only came into contact with this great Austrian carol as an adult. I recorded it for my first Christmas album as an adult with Universal Records and the melody is exquisite to sing. Its words may be monotonous, the first line of every verse being the same, so it's either 'Still, still, still' or, in the original, 'Sleep, sleep, sleep/Dream, dream, dream'. We changed the words for my album to the version above. I don't understand why this carol is not more popular, it should be taught in every school.

'Still, Still, Still' is also very easy to sing, no difficult parts at all. The third line of every verse is the most drawn out and gives the opportunity to really open out with the voice. My favourite line is the fourth, it's the highlight of the piece if you like, starting by being very, very quiet, very still and building up to all the light of heaven shining and the holy star telling this incredible news.

I performed this carol on *Songs of Praise* and the producer had the

STILL, STILL, STILL

139

idea of my being in a primary school in the dead of night. So all you see is me walking from classroom to classroom. It was filmed over a very long period of time, with the camera on a track so that it could pull back through the school. The children were preparing for Christmas but they weren't there: in the depths of the night it was very still and there was just one lone figure walking in this place.

It was wonderful seeing how much expectancy of Jesus coming into the world there was in that one primary school. They had brightly coloured paintings around the walls, Christmas trees in the corners, streamers everywhere. During the day it would have been full of merriment, laughter and energy; in deepest night it was eerily quiet, which was perfect for this carol.

In my particular recording of 'Still, Still, Still' I play around with the musical arrangement of the third and fourth lines of the third verse, and the melody I created really does seem to work with this carol. This is the carol's highlight, leading from the simplicity of 'Light, light, light/ The sky is filled with light', into hope with 'The holy star its news a-blazing'. I can't praise this carol enough. It would probably be in my top three.

I've heard many choirs do this, as well as solo performances, and one of the most momentous for me was listening to Bryn Terfel singing it in the Royal Albert Hall. Here was a giant of a man with a huge, huge voice effortlessly singing this motionless carol. He didn't move, his arms were by his sides all the way through, and out of his mouth just came this glorious voice singing this mesmeric carol.

27

THE SUSSEX CAROL

'On Christmas Night All Christians Sing'

WORDS AND MUSIC
Anon.

On Christmas night all Christians sing
To hear the news the angels bring:
News of great joy, news of great mirth,
News of our merciful King's birth.

Then why should men on earth be so sad,
Since our Redeemer made us glad
When from our sin he set us free,
All for to gain our liberty?

When sin departs before his grace,
Then life and health come in its place.
Angels and men with joy may sing,
All for to see the new-born King.

All out of darkness we have light,
Which made the angels sing this night:
'Glory to God and peace to men,
Now and for evermore, Amen'.

Also known as 'On Christmas Night All Christians Sing' or 'On Christmas Night True Christians Sing', this carol tells how all Christians rejoice at the coming of their Redeemer and their salvation – and the minute you start singing it, it puts a smile on your face.

'The Sussex Carol' first appeared in print as 'Another short carol for Christmas Day' by Luke Wadding, a seventeenth-century Irish bishop, in his *Smale Garland of Pious and Godly Songs*, which he published in 1684 shortly after his consecration to the diocese of Ferns, County Wexford. Otherwise, there is little known about Luke Wadding's life and we don't even know whether he wrote the carol himself; it's more likely that he recorded an earlier composition from medieval sources. Versions of the carol differing considerably from Wadding's original text appeared in print in both 1790 and 1847.

William Studwell, writing about 'The Sussex Carol', is puzzled by the English 'curious custom of naming some of their folk carols after the places of their supposed origin'. There are no such things as 'Provençal Carol', 'Catalan Carol', or 'Kentucky Carol', he points out. Well, yes, we do this, often recognising the place where a carol has its roots, or where it was first performed. In this book, for instance, there's the 'Coventry Carol', so-named because it was part of the Coventry Mystery Cycle. To be found as well, leafing through the literature, there's the bucolically titled 'Exeter Boar's Head Carol', various wassails, including 'The Somerset Wassail', 'The Gloucestershire Wassail' and more. Writers and composers of hymns and carols too, often name their compositions after a place in Britain that has special meaning for the words or tune. This was also the habit of Ralph Vaughan Williams' *An Oxford Elegy, On Wenlock Edge*. 'The Sussex Carol' was discovered in Sussex and written down by Vaughan Williams and Cecil Sharp, who heard it being sung by Mrs Harriet Verrall of Monks Gate. Vaughan Williams really loved Christmas and had a lifelong passion for carols, for their freshness, beauty and nobility, an enthusiasm that came from the pleasure he took in folk songs. He understood that these were being undermined by increasing

literacy and printed music in rural areas, so in an attempt to halt the decline of the folk song, he and Sharp, the founding father of the folklore tradition in England, travelled the length and breadth of the countryside collecting hymns and carols from the noted singers of the time like Harriet Verrall, transcribed them and in so doing preserved them.

It is not known where the version sung by Harriet Verrall to Cecil Sharp and Ralph Vaughan Williams came from and the words she sang differ widely from the original recorded by Wadding. However, it is this version that was printed in the *Journal of the Folk-Song Society* in 1905 and has since been taken up by many carol books including *The Oxford Book of Carols* of 1924. In this respect 'The Sussex Carol' is similar to other carols in the history of its origins – there is no true agreed original, rather, the provenance of the words and music is a process of various adaptations from different sources, chance encounters and timely publication. This is especially true of carols with folk origins, such as 'The Sussex Carol' and 'Deck the Hall'.

The history of the tune we now sing to the 'Sussex Carol' is also unknown. Although the text has been found with many tunes, the one that has become standard is 'Christmas Night', which Harriet Verrall used. Vaughan Williams took it down and arranged it for unaccompanied singing in 1920 with seven other traditional carols. He must have been impressed by Harriet Verrall – he also heard her sing 'Who Would True Valour See' to the stirring tune of 'Monks Gate' – a melody named after a place – which he also arranged for congregational singing. 'The Sussex Carol' does not have a standard refrain – instead, each verse comprises two couplets. The first is repeated, usually performed in unison voices. The second couplet is sung once in harmony, usually with three or four voices.

Harriet Verrall lived with her husband Peter in Monks Gate, later moving to Horsham. She seems to have possessed the largest store of songs around that area. Her husband was also a singer and they often sang to each other for their own pleasure by the fire in the evenings. Harriet Verrall died in 1918 aged sixty-three and Peter Verrall a few years

later. In the *The West Sussex Village Book*, Tony Wales mentions that the Verralls were buried together in an unmarked grave in Hills Cemetery, Horsham.

I often wondered, both as a chorister and then as an adult, whether, if Ralph Vaughan Williams hadn't heard Harriet Verrall singing this beautiful melody, 'The Sussex Carol' would have been lost to us forever. But this has to be one of my favourite carol melodies because it's so immediately appealing. It's got a great lilting rhythm and it's also pretty simple in its structure. There are great arrangements from David Willcocks and also Philip Ledger, both of King's College, Cambridge and I don't think there are any other great arrangements, not compared to those anyway.

I think it's a carol that you don't have to be a massively strong believer to get the most out of. It's to the point and cleverly written. Each verse tells a mini story in its own right and you don't need more than four verses to tell the whole story through to the final verse:

> All out of darkness we have light,
> Which made the angels sing this night:
> 'Glory to God and peace to men,
> Now and for evermore, Amen.'

I don't think it can get any better really, we have light and because of that the angels are singing and just to cap it off we get the final two lines, and 'Amen'!

It's difficult sometimes to get the most out of fast-paced carols vocally and in terms of performance, but this one is totally different. You have the instant gently swinging melody in the first two lines and then in the second two lines of each verse you really open out and express more through the voice and also the phrasing really comes into its own in those third and fourth lines. It's not one I've recorded thus far but all that's about to change with the release of my Christmas album, 2010, and this one is definitely among the first on the list. It's a carol that also works tremendously well with brass accompaniment, which we've had on *Songs*

of Praise quite a few times. I don't know why, but there's something quite magical about the congregation singing a Christmas carol like this one with the brass alongside. It's almost as if the music brings you closer to Heaven.

THE SUSSEX
CAROL

145

28

THE FIRST NOWELL

WORDS AND MUSIC Traditional Cornish carol

Adapted and arranged by Davies Gilbert (1767–1839)

The first Nowell the angel did say
Was to certain poor shepherds in fields as they lay;
In fields where they lay keeping their sheep
On a cold winter's night that was so deep.

Nowell, nowell, nowell. nowell!
Born is the King of Israel.

They looked up and saw a star,
Shining in the east, beyond them far;
And to the earth it gave great light,
And so it continued both day and night.

Refrain

And by the light of that same star,
Three wise men came from country far;
To seek for a King was their intent
And to follow the star wherever it went.

Refrain

This star drew nigh to the north-west
O'er Bethlehem it took its rest,
And there it did both stop and stay
Right over the place where Jesus lay.

Refrain

Then entered in those wise men three,
Full reverently, upon their knee,
And offered there in his presence
Their gold and myrrh and frankincense.

Refrain

Then let us all with one accord
Sing praises to our Heavenly Lord,
That hath made heaven and earth of naught,
And with his blood mankind hath bought.

Refrain.

Nowell is from the French 'Noël', meaning Christmas of course, and this is one of those carols which, if you didn't hear it at Christmas, you would feel you'd missed out. It's among a handful that the choir does breathing, or sleeping, or eating: it's Christmas and you hear 'O Come, All Ye Faithful', 'Hark! The Herald Angels Sing', 'Silent Night' – and 'The First Nowell'.

Together the shepherds of St Luke's Gospel and the wise men of Matthew's book follow the light of the travelling star. It is likely that this carol first appeared in 1823 in Davies Gilbert's *Some Ancient Christmas Carols*. It next appeared ten years later in William Sandys' (1792–1874) volume of *Christmas Carols Ancient and Modern*, published in 1833. Both marked the beginning of many such collections by editors who were contributing to the new kind of Victorian fireside Christmas that came about over the following decades of the nineteenth century.

But 'The First Nowell' has medieval beginnings, possibly as far back as the thirteenth century, and the version we are familiar with is thought to be of Cornish origin. Some regions of England – Cornwall in particular – have developed their own carol tradition. In his introduction to *Lyver Canow Kernewek* (*The Cornish Song Book*, published in 1929), Ralph Dunstan describes various groups of Cornish carols, notably folk carols, the Redruth-Camborne Carols sung in mining communities across the county, and that good old catch-all, 'miscellaneous'. 'The First Nowell' may well belong to a variant going back to medieval tunes in Cornwall. Dunstan comments that the words for 'The First Nowell' in his collection come from an old Cornish broadside that, printed in Helston, was hawked around the county by pedlars for a halfpenny. He remembers actually seeing one of these stuck on cottage walls near his home.

Davies Gilbert, who collected the version known today, was born Davies Giddy. He later changed his surname to that of his wife Mary-Anne in order to inherit her uncle's estate in Sussex (the contents included shells, fossils, a telescope, conversation stools and a ewe in a glass case).

Gilbert's love of the history and culture of Cornwall fuelled his knowledge of ancient songs from that county and has meant that carols such as 'The First Nowell' have been preserved for so many generations. In his preface to the collection, Gilbert pointed out that carols had been sung in private homes on Christmas Eve and on Christmas Day in the churches throughout the West of England up to the end of the eighteenth century – when carol singing in England was otherwise out of fashion and favour. He wanted to preserve them complete with any false grammar, 'as specimens of times now passed away, and of religious feelings superseded by others of a different cast'. This is not an unusual motivation for carol collectors, including the great Percy Dearmer, but on a more personal note, Gilbert also wrote that he was preserving them as well because they had given him such childhood delight: 'On Christmas

Eve at seven or eight o'clock in the evening cakes were drawn hot from the oven; cyder or beer exhilarated the spirits in every house; and the singing of Carols was continued late into the night.' As Davies Gilbert intended, 'The First Nowell' can take us back to the 'delights' of a magical childhood Christmas; it's a song about the wonder of the Nativity that many of us have sung.

Davies Gilbert died on Christmas Eve 1879 aged seventy-two years. He had lived a life full of energy and activity. He was by no means a typical hymn collector, being an engineer and a scientist, and sometime President of the Royal Society of Science. He also found the time to be Member of Parliament for Helston (where he grew up) and then Bodmin over twenty-eight years. He was a writer too; maybe it's a sign of the breadth of his knowledge, and typical of the polymath age in which he lived, that he published (a strong candidate for the most unusual, certainly the longest book title of the year) *On the vibrations of heavy bodies in cycloidal and in circular arches, as compared with their descents through free space; including an estimate of the variable circular excess in vibrations continually decreasing*!

'The First Nowell' is not short of critics. Comprising what is, without much variation, basically one tune in the verse that's repeated in the refrain, there's reason to wonder whether the melody is one section of another tune. Possibly it was the treble part that, lost in transcription, was mistaken for the main melody. One idea was that the words for 'The First Nowell' were once sung to the tune for 'On Christmas Night All Christians Sing' and they do fit the music for this carol.

The question of how many shepherds there were has created confusion. The Gospel does not specifically state that there were three, while some legends speak of four. In the medieval mystery play *Play of the Shepherds* there are four, called – rather like Hobbits or Shakespeare's rude mechanicals – Harvey, Tudd, Trowle and Hancken.

Putting aside these doubts and debates, it's an inspiring carol often chosen for services at Christmas. It was in the line-up for the first Nine Lessons and Carols at King's College, Cambridge in 1918 when it was sung after the Ninth Lesson and on another occasion placed after the

Seventh. It was a carol I first performed in Bangor Cathedral during my time as a chorister there.

'The First Nowell' was one of several that British composer Christian Victor Hely-Hutchinson, born on Boxing Day in 1901 (died 1947), used for his 'Carol Symphony', noted for its opening variation on the theme of 'The First Nowell'. Fans of John Masefield will know it as the music for the BBC's 1984 television adaptation of his *Box of Delights* and for radio's *Children's Hour* dramatisation, broadcast both during and just after the Second World War. It's been recorded by many artists, from Bing Crosby on his *White Christmas* album through to Bob Dylan on his 2009 seasonal *Christmas in the Heart*. I've also heard it performed by the Australian children's group the Wiggles.

This is what you call a 'crowd-pleasing carol'. Due to the repetitive way in which it's constructed I suppose the melody does stick instantly in the mind. Again as with many carols, it's a Big Sing. There are lots and lots of verses – no one's suggesting that you do all of them otherwise you'd be in performance all night. I think it's also one of those carols where, though it's slightly overlong, the refrain absolutely does save it. It gives the congregation an opportunity to really, really sing out 'Nowell, Nowell, Nowell, Nowell/Born is the King of Israel'. It doesn't get simpler, but that simplicity gives you the opportunity through voice to praise God and the chorus is quite majestic and to the point.

I'm about to record 'The First Nowell' on my new Christmas album and I have to say it's with some trepidation, because I'm not sure how I can maintain interest throughout and I'm still not sure whether it will work as a solo piece because it needs that whole congregational input. When you hear the organ accompaniment start and everyone stands up, you're sure you're on safe ground. It's one of those carols that has seeped into your bloodstream, it's in your heart, it's in your soul, you don't really have to think when you are performing it. I suppose there's a lot to be said for that.

29

SILENT NIGHT!

(Stille Nacht!)

WORDS
Joseph Mohr (1792–1848)

MUSIC
Franz Xaver Gruber (1787–1863)

SILENT NIGHT!

151

Silent night! Holy night!
All is calm, all is bright.
Round yon virgin mother and child,
Holy infant so tender and mild,
Sleep in heavenly peace,
Sleep in heavenly peace.

Silent night! Holy night!
Shepherds quake at the sight.
Glories stream from heaven afar,
Heavenly hosts sing Alleluia
Christ the Saviour is born!
Christ the Saviour is born!

Silent night! Holy night!
Son of God, love's pure light.
Radiant beams from thy holy face
With the dawn of redeeming grace,
Jesus, Lord, at thy birth.
Jesus, Lord, at thy birth.

Silent night

J. Mohr

F. Gruber

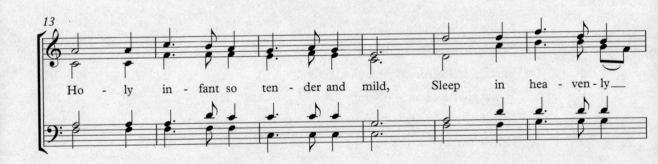

From the little town of Oberndorf where it was composed to Tahiti and Greenland, Latvia and Taiwan, 'Stille Nacht!', 'Silent Night!' is the world's most popular carol. It has been translated into at least 250 languages, arranged for many instruments and is an essential part of Christmas.

'Silent Night!' so often wins surveys of Britain's favourite carols that its place at the top is pretty stable; it was also the favourite of twenty-one per cent of entries to a December 1996 Gallup poll, way ahead of the runners-up 'Away in a Manger' and 'O Come, All Ye Faithful'. A hard one to beat.

How 'Stille Nacht!' came to be written is a fine, if fictional, tale. On Christmas Eve 1818 the organ in the parish church of the little Lower Austrian (now Bavarian) church of Oberndorf had given up the ghost. Presented with a list of carols for his congregation and no organ accompaniment, the enterprising curate Joseph Mohr (who played the guitar) and assistant organist Franz Xaver Gruber between them quickly wrote a carol to be sung at midnight mass on Christmas Eve with guitar accompaniment. Various interpretations of the reason for the organ's temporary disablement include rust and the nibbles of a mouse at the organ's cables. The mouse's point of view on the creation of 'Stille Nacht!' has been dramatized on TV, narrated by actress Lynn Redgrave.

Sadly, this story doesn't add up. There's a manuscript in Joseph Mohr's handwriting that shows he actually wrote the words to the simple poem 'Stille Nacht!' in 1816, while he was a curate in the Austrian alps, inspired by the little villages peppering the surrounding mountains, peaceful and lit by the stars.

'Stille Nacht!' is an Austrian/Bavarian folk song for the midnight service. Like 'Rocking Carol', it would have been sung by the crib placed in the church for the Christmas period. It certainly has the calm, spiritual quality of a lullaby. There are many such songs, but what Mohr and Gruber did was produce a carol that has captivated countless people's hearts from then to now.

The story continues with Gruber, a kind and trusting man, liberally

distributing copies of his carol, often without bothering to add his name to it. One of these came into the hands of a glove-maker and folk-music enthusiast Josef Strasser. He was part of the family Strasser singing group, who performed the carol as a 'Tyrolean folk carol', newly unearthed. Sounds familiar . . . Tyrol . . . family singing group . . . In fact the Von Trapp family singers of Robert Wise's *The Sound of Music* (1965) won the music festival presented in the film in Salzburg, a few miles from Oberndorf.

The Strassers sang the carol at a concert in Leipzig in December 1832 and it was published by an A R Friese, as the last of his 'Four Authentic Tyrolean Songs' for soprano soloist or four voices with optional piano accompaniment. Mohr and Gruber had to turn to the law and the courts to reclaim the authorship of *Stille Nacht!*.

Joseph Mohr was born in Salzburg on 11 December 1792. His mother was poor, a young woman making a meagre living as an embroiderer when she met his father Franz Mohr, a soldier, who abandoned her, one imagines, when he learned she was pregnant. It wasn't easy for an illegitimate boy to make his way in the world, but Joseph's musical talents were recognised; he chose the religious life, and was ordained in 1815. As curate for the pilgrimage church at Mariapfarr in the Austrian Alps, he wrote the six-stanza poem that became 'Stille Nacht!' and while priest at St Nicholas, he befriended Franz Gruber, a local teacher who was also assistant organist in the church, and together priest and organist composed 'Stille Nacht!' Gruber, the son of linen weavers, born in Hochburg in Upper Austria, who dedicated most of his life to church music as choir director, singer and organist, described 'Stille Nacht!' as 'a simple composition'.

First translated into English around 1858 by Emily Elliott for St Mark's Church in Brighton as 'Stilly night, holy night', the carol has since had many translations. Minister and hymn-writer John Freeman Young (1820–85) of Pittston, Maine, is credited with translating the three-verse carol that is most widely sung today.

Popular in America, 'Silent Night!' was for a time considered vulgar

in England and omitted from most books of hymns and carols. Bing Crosby came to the rescue and brought it to millions when he sang 'Silent Night!' in the 1945 film *The Bells of St Mary's*.

'Silent Night!' has been performed by a multitude of other artists in just about every musical genre. Enya sang it in Irish, Andrea Bocelli in Italian, Mahalia Jackson gave it the gospel treatment, Fleetwood Mac's Stevie Nicks sang it solo. Mannheim Steamroller, the group founded by Chip Davis and known for their modern renditions of Christmas carols, recorded an instrumental version, and on their *Parsley, Sage, Rosemary and Thyme* album, Simon and Garfunkel recorded their own offering, '7 o'clock News/Silent Night'. Here they sing the carol to the accompaniment of items reporting murders, and a newscast about the Vietnam War. The beauty of the singing and the song, backed by broadcast news of death and destruction, is particularly disturbing.

Going back to the beginning of this lovely carol, St Nicholas's Church in Oberndorf was demolished in the early twentieth century. A little 'Silent Night Memorial Chapel' now stands on the site. On that spot and throughout the world in hundreds of languages, 'Heavenly hosts sing Alleluia' for 'Christ the Saviour is born'.

'Silent Night!' is another one I've performed since I was at school and definitely in Bangor Cathedral. I think it comes into its own when sung as a solo piece. You really do feel that you have more of a connection with the Nativity itself and with God when sung solo. I've done it as a duet with Hayley Westenra in concert and with choirs; I've performed it with orchestra and, as an adult, on my third album. I really do think that when you strip away this carol, it truly comes into its own and these days all you really need is a guitar accompaniment, which is exactly how it was composed. So I'm very thankful to the mouse for eating away at the organ pipes.

Recently on the ITV celebration of Christmas I went out to Israel and explored some of the stories behind the carols. I was very fortunate to mime 'Silent Night!', not out in Israel, which was where most of the programme was done, but in Flanders, where so many British soldiers

SILENT NIGHT!

155

had lost their lives in World War I. By all accounts this carol was sung in the trenches, in no man's land. There was a truce for a matter of moments, where the German and the British soldiers stopped fighting and eerily all you heard coming across no man's land in the bitter cold, in a time of desperation, were the German troops singing 'Stille Nacht!' and coming back at them was 'Good King Wenceslas' from the British soldiers. Two fighting armies had been hard at it trying to kill one another and then, because it was Christmas, they decided to stop and they played a game of football and sang carols. Such is the power of a carol like this that when I was there in Flanders I could actually begin to imagine what it was like for those soldiers. In the middle of so much hatred and brutality something as beautiful as 'Stille Nacht!' was sung.

My first live performance of 'Stille Nacht!' was on German television when I was a young child in the prime of my boy chorister career. I went over there with my accompanist from Wales, Annette Bryn Parry, probably one of the finest accompanists ever to have come out of Wales. We really were on holiday in our hotel, playing table tennis together, going swimming, and we were to perform on the number one TV show in Germany, which had interviews, a game show element, a panel of people talking – and lots of different music. On that particular programme the London Community Gospel Choir were also performing. I was there to sing 'Stille Nacht!' in German, with Annette accompanying on a very, very dodgy keyboard, which they provided for us.

Well, being used to television in Britain and being looked after by a German representative, there was no rush getting to the rehearsal. She remarked that, 'Oh, just like British television, we'll be running late.' We arrived ten minutes late for the rehearsal and the producer came running up to me (I was only thirteen at the time) and berated me for my lateness. He said, 'We're not going to let you rehearse any more because you don't take it seriously.' I was bright red, mortified, because even at that age I really did pride myself on being a professional; after all, I'd been told there was no rush to get to the rehearsal. So I apologised, grovelled – a lot – and gave the performance of my life on the live broadcast of the show.

The following week, I was sitting next to Boy George – as you do – at a rock and pop awards event in London at the Grosvenor Hotel and I regaled him with this tale. And he said, 'Oh, I was on that programme the week before – they did the same thing to me. I turned round to them and said, "If you don't let me rehearse, I'm going" and took the next plane home.' This I think is the difference between me and Boy George: I grovelled in the classical style, saying 'I'm terribly sorry, I'll do a good performance for you, promise!' Whereas Boy George, in rock 'n' roll style, turned round and said, 'Sod you all, I'm off.'

My favourite verse, without doubt, has to be the third. It gives you the opportunity to open up with the voice on the first two lines:

> Silent night! Holy night!
> Son of God, love's pure light.

Then I always in performance take the third line back in dynamic completely with

> Radiant beams from thy holy face
> With the dawn of redeeming grace,
> Jesus, Lord, at thy birth,
> Jesus, Lord, at thy birth.

That's a kind of moment between me and God when I'm performing the carol. It's a one-on-one if you like. I feel that I'm connecting with that one person. It's the beauty of this carol that it can be enjoyed by the masses, but actually when I'm performing it, selfishly I feel that it's a piece of music where I have this connection with God.

30

WHILE SHEPHERDS WATCHED
THEIR FLOCKS BY NIGHT

Words
Nahum Tate (1652–1715)

Music
Arrangement by
William Henry Monk (1823–89)

While shepherds watched their flocks by night,
All seated on the ground,
The angel of the Lord came down,
And glory shone around.

'Fear not,' said he (for mighty dread
Had seized their troubled minds),
'Glad tidings of great joy I bring
To you and all mankind.

'To you in David's town this day
Is born of David's line
A Saviour, who is Christ the Lord;
And this shall be the sign:

'The heavenly babe you there shall find
To human view displayed,
All meanly wrapped in swathing bands,
And in a manger laid.'

Thus spake the seraph; and forthwith
Appeared a shining throng

Of angels praising God, and thus
Addressed their joyful song:

'All glory be to God on high,
And to the earth be peace;
Good will henceforth from heaven to men,
Begin and never cease.'

Together, the carols in this book tell the Christmas story more or less from beginning to end. The central themes and happenings are here – and some subplots as well. Isaiah's prophecy of the coming of Emmanuel features, so do Herod's nefarious schemes and the coming of the three kings. The journey to Bethlehem on a little donkey and the birth in the stable are of course included: Mary, Joseph and baby, surrounded by Magi, shepherds and sheep, an ox, an ass, even in Christina Rossetti's carol – a camel! And the story continues through the massacre of the innocents and the Holy Family's flight into Egypt.

The shepherds in particular crop up frequently. In 'See Amid the Winter's Snow', for instance, they talk about following the star to find Jesus; in 'The First Nowell', the selfsame star guides them and the three kings to the stable in Bethlehem, and in 'The Shepherds' Farewell' they see off the Holy Family on their journey back home with words of encouragement and comfort. The shepherds of Christmas refer maybe to Christ the Good Shepherd; they perhaps also represent us, ordinary human beings, members of congregations and choirs, a flock, and never more so than in this carol. These shepherds are simple folk, who are scared stiff when the angel of the Lord swoops down in a blaze of light giving them headline news. 'Fear not,' he admonishes, then brings along a terrifying throng of singing angels. Quite an event for an ordinary shepherd to deal with.

First published in 1700, 'While Shepherds Watched their Flocks by Night' comes from Luke's Gospel (2:8–14) when that angel appears to the

shepherds resting in the field and gives them 'glad tidings of great joy' of the coming of Christ. Popular – and parodied – it tells a story and the angel speaks directly to the shepherds and to us, a rare thing in a carol. This directness maybe contributes to its appeal as one of our most popular carols, and it's clear and simple for children to sing with joy.

'While Shepherds Watched their Flocks by Night' is also one of England's earliest carols. From the beginning of the sixteenth until the eighteenth century, the singing of hymns and carols was practically non-existent in most of England. Instead, church congregations sang versified forms of the Psalms, which came to be considered rather crude and un-poetic in nature. In 1696, two Irishmen, Nahum Tate and Nicholas Brady, collaborated to undertake a new metrical version of the Psalms with higher literary standards than hitherto. It was Nahum Tate, one half of this partnership, who wrote 'While Shepherds Watched Their Flocks by Night', paraphrasing Luke's verses. The Anglican Church accepted his work and for eighty-two years it was the only carol that had the church's stamp of approval, until 'Hark! The Herald Angels Sing' was added to the approved list in 1782.

Nahum Tate was the son of an Irish clergyman who went by the name of Faithful Teate. Unsurprisingly Nahum changed his surname to Tate when he moved to England. He was considered to be a distinguished if eccentric poet and writer for the stage and John Dryden was his friend. His achievements for the stage included adapting a libretto for Henry Purcell's opera *Dido and Aeneas*. He also had the curious habit of rewriting Shakespeare's plays. His version of the tragedy of *King Lear* had a happy ending, with Cordelia alive and well and married to Edgar; he also changed *Richard II* so that every scene, he said, was 'full of respect to Majesty and the dignity of courts'. This didn't seem to worry his contemporaries and he was made Poet Laureate in 1692. But he fell victim to excessive drinking and died in 1715 in Southwark, where he had taken refuge from his creditors.

Many small changes have successively been made to the original text of 'While Shepherds Watched their Flocks by Night'. The 'swathing

bands' of verse four, for example, have been substituted by the more modern 'swaddling clothes' or 'swaddling bands'. In Scotland there is a completely different first verse:

> While humble shepherds watched their flocks
> In Bethlehem's plains by night
> An angel sent from heaven appeared
> And filled the plains with light.

Another variation sometimes performed is 'As shepherds watched their fleecy care'. Like children before and since, I was guilty as a child in school of parodying this carol many times:

> While shepherds washed their socks at night
> All seated round the tub,
> A bar of Sunlight soap came down
> And they began to scrub.

Or alternatively:

> While shepherds washed their socks by night
> And hung them on the line,
> The angel of the Lord came down
> And said, 'Those socks are mine!'

I remember being told off quite severely at Bangor Cathedral as a relatively new chorister when I nudged my compatriots and dared them to sing the sock-washing variant. I feel sorry now for the choirmaster of the time because he'd been there for many, many years and every Christmas must have lived in dread of some smart chorister coming out with the wisecrack of singing the alternative words – very boring.

The number of competing tunes for this carol must be a record. An estimated 100-plus have appeared in print. One of the most popular is

'Winchester Old', a psalm tune first published in 1592 and arranged by William Henry Monk some time before 1874, popular perhaps because its strong beats convey the rhythm of Tate's words and it has a fine descant. Monk was an important person in the history of hymnody, being the first ever musical editor of the highly influential first collection of *Hymns Ancient and Modern* of 1861 – a bestseller that has sold millions through its successive editions. He made his living as organist for churches across the map of London, including St Peter's Church in Eaton Square, and St Paul's Church, Portman Square, and was organist and choirmaster at St Matthias' Church in Stoke Newington. But he was also composer of memorable hymns and carols. He wrote the tune to Cecil Frances Alexander's 'All Things Bright and Beautiful' and the lovely 'Eventide' for 'Abide with Me', as well as a selection of other melodies including the oddly-titled 'Martyrdom' by Hugh Wilson in 1800 and 'Shackelford' by Frederick Henry Cheeswright in 1889. A parish organist in Lancashire, Robert Jackson, wrote 'Jackson's Tune' for the carol and that remains popular there. In Cornwall the carol is popularly sung to 'Lyngham', a tune usually associated with 'O For A Thousand Tongues to Sing!' and many other tunes are still sung to Tate's words by village carollers in Yorkshire, most notably 'Foster' or rather, 'Old Foster', more like a couple of ales, which maybe explains why 'While Shepherds Watched their Flocks by Night' is carolled particularly in local pubs!

Even though the melody is really nice to sing and the words are wonderful, 'While Shepherds Watched their Flocks by Night' is not among my favourites; it's neither one thing nor the other. It doesn't quite hit the majesty and grandeur of 'O Come All Ye Faithful' or 'Hark! The Herald Angels Sing', nor is it a mood-enhancing carol. It is what it is. Some of the verses can be quite clumsy; the only one I really enjoyed singing as a boy was the third:

> 'To you in David's town this day
> Is born of David's line
> A Saviour, who is Christ the Lord;
> And this shall be the sign:

This is, though, what you'd call a perfect congregation carol, a carol to get everyone singing. It's instantly recognisable, it's one that anyone in Britain has sung at some point during a school assembly and it is testament to the words and the melody that you probably have to hear it only a couple of times and you feel that you know it. Lots of the carols in this anthology itself would love this to be the truth about them.

'While Shepherds Watched' really did come to life for me recently when I had the opportunity of performing it out in Israel. I was sitting in the shepherds' fields and we'd been filming for quite a while and the sun was just setting and there was one particular recording we did as dusk fell when I really did feel what a privilege it was to be in the fields in Israel where the shepherds would have been when they experienced what they did. It was quite a surreal experience. I almost re-lived the second verse and imagined how I would feel if an angel came down while I was sitting there minding my own business, so it always puts a smile on my face now when I hear

> 'Fear not,' said he (for mighty dread
> Had seized their troubled minds),

It's as if they see the angel, they panic like mad and the angel says, 'Hey, don't worry, I'm only here because I've got some good news for you.' They go, 'Oh that's fine then, fire away.' I'm not sure that my head would be so easily turned, I think that that angel would have had to explain a lot more.

I think all of these carols that are simple in their telling of a story should be commended for the fact that their creators can actually tell the story of the Nativity, probably the greatest story in the world, in four or five short stanzas – this is a real testament to their writing skills.

31

THE SHEPHERDS' FAREWELL TO THE HOLY FAMILY

WORDS
Anon.

TRANSLATION
Paul England (dates not known)

MUSIC
Hector Berlioz (1803–69)

Thou must leave thy lowly dwelling,
The humble crib, the stable bare.
Babe, all mortal babes excelling,
Content our earthly lot to share.

Loving father, loving mother,
Shelter thee with tender care.
Loving father, loving mother,
Shelter thee with tender care,
Shelter thee with tender care.

Blessed Jesus, we implore thee
With humble love and holy fear,
In the land that lies before thee,
Forget not us who linger here.

May the shepherd's lowly calling
Ever to thy heart be dear.
May the shepherd's lowly calling

Ever to thy heart be dear,
Ever to thy heart be dear.

Blest are ye beyond all measure,
Thou happy father, mother mild;
Guard ye well your heav'nly treasure,
The Prince of peace, the holy child.

God go with you, God protect you,
Guide you safely through the wild.
God go with you, God protect you,
Guide you safely through the wild,
Guide you safely through the wild.

This is an intimate song of the shepherds voicing their love and concern for the Holy Family who are leaving Bethlehem to escape Herod's wrath. It's achingly beautiful, but in a great way so that you can really put your heart and soul into singing it.

It is a short work for orchestra and chorus that's part of a larger choral oratorio by Hector Berlioz, called *L'Enfance du Christ*. Berlioz was a key figure of his time, friend of Victor Hugo and Alexandre Dumas, and a champion of Beethoven, then unheard of in France. His father wanted him to become a doctor and he spent two unsuccessful years fulfilling his father's wishes and training in medicine before performing his own flight into music.

Oddly for such a meditative composition, 'The Shepherds' Farewell' began life as a stand-alone piece and a party joke and was the seed from which grew one of Hector Berlioz's finest works. By the age of forty-seven he had become frustrated with the reluctance of audiences and critics to appreciate the modernist nature of his music. To his chagrin they considered it to be discordant and bizarre. This lack of recognition was more than irritating; it meant he had no regular income and was extremely hard up. In October 1850, Berlioz had written a short organ piece for the autograph album of his friend the architect Joseph-Louis Duc, under the fictitious name of Pierre Ducré. He reworked this piece to his own text as '*L'adieu des bergers a la Sainte Famille*' or 'The Shepherds' Farewell to the Holy Family'. He then decided to trick the critics and the audience by passing off 'The Shepherds' Farewell' as a tune 'in the antique style' by this fictitious seventeenth-century composer Pierre Ducré and supposedly written in the year 1679. His plan worked. He conducted the work on 12 November, at a concert of the Grande Société Philharmonique de Paris and it was enthusiastically received by all. His British biographer David Cairns observes that Berlioz was told by Joseph-Louis Duc that 'a society lady of his acquaintance, a connoisseur of ancient music, had declared that "Berlioz would never be able to write a tune as simple and charming as this little piece by old Ducré."'

Nonetheless the cool response to Berlioz's work continued. Many put the success of 'The Shepherds' Farewell' down to a change of style adopted by Berlioz to win approval. He was at pains to point out that any change was due to the touching subject matter and nothing else. In a postscript to his memoirs he explains:

> In that work many people imagined they could detect a radical change in my style and manner. This opinion is entirely without foundation. The subject naturally lent itself to a gentle and simple style of music, and for that reason alone was more in accordance with their taste and intelligence. Time would probably have developed these qualities, but I should have written *L'Enfance du Christ* in the same manner twenty years ago. (*J'eusse écrit* L'Enfance du Christ *de la même façon il y a vingt ans.*)

Berlioz described *L'Enfance du Christ*, the oratorio of which 'The Shepherds' Farewell' was the seed, as a *trilogie sacrée* (sacred trilogy). It tells the story of Herod's genocide and Mary and Joseph's painful and arduous flight to Egypt to take refuge in the city of Sais. Berlioz took his narrative from

the second chapter of the book of Matthew, and composed what many consider to be one of his gentlest and most endearing scores. Untypically he specified a smaller orchestral force than usual. 'The Shepherds' Farewell' comes in the second section, 'The Flight into Egypt', which is itself divided into three parts. Berlioz added a tenor part *Le repos de la Sainte Famille* ('The repose of the Holy Family') and then set an overture before both this and the original 'Shepherds' Farewell' to form what we know now as *La fuite en Egypte*.

The writing of the three-part oratorio did not start at the very beginning. 'The Flight into Egypt' was published in 1852 and performed in December the following year at Leipzig. This was so well received that, on the advice of his friends, Berlioz added more to his composition, topping and tailing it with the last section *L'arrivée a Sais* and finally the opening section, *Le songe d'Hérode* ('Herod's Dream'). The entire sacred trilogy took four years to complete.

Berlioz was married twice, the first time to the Irish actress Harriet Smithson (1800–54) who inspired his *Symphonie Fantastique* written in 1830. They had a son, Louis, born in 1834. Louis' death in 1867 was a terrible blow to his father who by then had already lost many of his friends and family. It prompted him to burn many of his papers, and he died only two years later.

Perhaps because Hector Berlioz turned to the music of other countries such as Britain and Germany for inspiration he is still to this day treated with some indifference in his native land. In 2003, two hundred years after his birth, it was proposed that his remains, buried between his two wives in the Cimetière de Montmartre, be moved to the Panthéon. This idea was blocked by Jacques Chirac, then President of France, because he considered it too soon after the body of Alexandre Dumas had been moved there. Opponents of the idea have come from different sides: some felt Berlioz was not a Republican, others that his wish to be beside his wives should be respected. The decision on this matter is still pending.

In the UK, affection for Berlioz is maybe due to the conductor Colin

Davies, who has recorded all of his work, including two renditions of *L'Enfance du Christ*, one on vinyl in 1977 with Janet Baker and a CD nearly thirty years later: a live recording with the London Symphony Orchestra and the chamber choir Tenebrae in December 2006.

This wonderful piece lasts little over five minutes. It depicts a deeply moving episode in the story of the Nativity, giving a vivid account of the shepherds gathering by the crib and bidding Jesus goodbye. They urge him not to forget their lowly selves and utter a prayer for Christ's safe future. It's all the more poignant because we know how unsafe that future will be. It's often sung as part of a carol service as well as within the oratorio to which it eventually came to belong.

I first sang this piece at Bangor Cathedral and it is a beautiful marriage of words and music, one that I'll be recording on my 2010 album for Christmas, I expect, as a duet between me and a choir.

I think it has probably one of the nicest carol melodies that we've got and it's not an obvious melody. I love the introduction: like the carol itself it's not conspicuous, it's very simple and is almost as if it is coming from a shepherd's pipe – the sound of the pipes and horns in the accompaniment too give it a sense of the pastoral. It's very, very simple and you don't really expect this searingly beautiful melody to come through, but then it does and it's just the most joyous piece to sing: open long phrases and sublime melody, especially during the end of each verse, where you repeat the last two lines. There the words are also at their strongest, so repeating them three times reinforces their message:

> Loving father, loving mother,
> Shelter thee with tender care,
> Loving father, loving mother,
> Shelter thee with tender care,
> Shelter thee with tender care.

I also love the final verse: 'God go with you, God protect you/ Guide you safely through the wild.'

I hear this carol every year as it's part of our charity event in St George's Hanover Square. I think this is one of the pieces of music that the Westminster Cathedral Choir do so well. Their exposed boys' voices at first, then joined by the male voices. They also sing it in French, and even if you're not fluent in French the meaning of the words comes across because it's so well written. Hearing a choir of top boys' voices singing it is a real treat for me at Christmas and I think it is one of the carols that really does set up the true meaning of the festival for me.

THE SHEPHERDS'
FAREWELL TO
THE HOLY FAMILY

32

THE TWELVE DAYS OF CHRISTMAS

WORDS AND MUSIC
Anon.

Musical arrangement by Frederic Austin (1872–1952)

On the first day of Christmas
My true love sent to me
A partridge in a pear tree.

On the second day of Christmas
My true love sent to me
Two turtle doves,
And a partridge in a pear tree.

On the third day of Christmas
My true love sent to me
Three French hens, Two turtle doves,
And a partridge in a pear tree.

On the fourth day of Christmas
My true love sent to me
Four calling birds, Three French hens,
Two turtle doves,
And a partridge in a pear tree.

On the fifth day of Christmas
My true love sent to me
Five gold rings, Four calling birds,
Three French hens, Two turtle doves,
And a partridge in a pear tree.

On the sixth day of Christmas
My true love sent to me
Six geese a-laying, Five gold rings,
Four calling birds, Three French hens, Two turtle doves,
And a partridge in a pear tree.

On the seventh day of Christmas
My true love sent to me
Seven swans a-swimming, Six geese a-laying,
Five gold rings, Four calling birds,
Three French hens, Two turtle doves,
And a partridge in a pear tree.

On the eighth day of Christmas
My true love sent to me
Eight maids a-milking, Seven swans a-swimming,
Six geese a-laying, Five gold rings,
Four calling birds, Three French hens, Two turtle doves,
And a partridge in a pear tree.

On the ninth day of Christmas
My true love sent to me
Nine ladies dancing, Eight maids a-milking,
Seven swans a-swimming, Six geese a-laying,
Five gold rings, Four calling birds, Three French hens, Two turtle doves,
And a partridge in a pear tree.

On the tenth day of Christmas
My true love sent to me
Ten lords a-leaping, Nine ladies dancing,
Eight maids a-milking, Seven swans a-swimming,
Six geese a-laying, Five gold rings, Four calling birds,
Three French hens, Two turtle doves,
And a partridge in a pear tree.

On the eleventh day of Christmas
My true love sent to me
Eleven pipers piping, Ten lords a-leaping,
Nine ladies dancing, Eight maids a-milking,
Seven swans a-swimming, Six geese a-laying,
Five gold rings, Four calling birds,
Three French hens, Two turtle doves,
And a partridge in a pear tree.

On the twelfth day of Christmas
My true love sent to me
Twelve drummers drumming, Eleven pipers piping,
Ten lords a-leaping, Nine ladies dancing,
Eight maids a-milking, Seven swans a-swimming,
Six geese a-laying, Five gold rings,
Four calling birds, Three French hens, Two turtle doves,
And a partridge in a pear tree.

'The Twelve Days of Christmas' belongs to those magical Christmases of childhood. It was a real treat for us at Bangor Cathedral if during the Christmas period we were allowed to sing this. One point we'd usually get to was a real joy because if you were an established chorister, you'd always look across at the probationers who were starting their life in the Cathedral choir and

didn't have a clue what the words were or how to keep them in time –
because it's quite a tricky song from that point of view – a choristers'
joke. But it was also a stressful sing for all of us. For the Nine Lessons
and Carols service we had three carol books to use and were constantly
flicking from one book to another, to another and another all through
the Nine Lessons and Carols. And invariably a chorister, usually me,
would drop a book or a page or a bookmark, much to the anger of
the choirmaster.

I've always loved this carol though because it portrays vivid pictures
in your mind. It's not every day you get to sing about turtle doves, or
maids a-milking, or lords a-leaping, or ladies dancing!

It's likely that the origin of 'The Twelve Days of Christmas', which
dates back at least to its first publication in England in 1780, was a festive
feat of memory and of maths to be sung by everyone together on Twelfth
Night (hence the twelve days), the feast of the Epiphany. A cumulative
song, it is often listed as a nursery rhyme and is a fine game, building as
it does from one item up to the twelve along with all the previous items
attached.

The words that we sing today were printed in 1864, but the earliest
known performance of the song was in 1842 by James Halliwell-Phillipps,
an English scholar. In the early twentieth century the composer Frederic
Austin, best known for his restoration and production of John Gay's *The
Beggar's Opera*, wrote an arrangement that included his own melody from
the verse 'Five gold rings' onwards. Austin's version has now become
standard.

A lot of people have speculated about the genesis of 'The Twelve
Days of Christmas', which is not an obviously religious carol. The real
meaning could be hidden within the verses like a code according to one
interpretation, each of the gifts holding religious significance. The 'true
love' of the carol is not a generous, if rather impractical, admirer, but is
God who gives wonderful gifts to 'me', meaning all of us. But why go to
the trouble of concealing these things deep in a Christmas song for
children? The hypothesis is that 'The Twelve Days of Christmas' was

created by Catholics during a time (1558–1829) when they were not allowed to practise their faith openly and when the only legal church was the state, Anglican, church. This song would not raise the suspicions of non-Catholics and the articles communicated in this way would help Catholic children growing up to remember central elements of their faith. The references suggested are:

- The partridge is a reminder of Christ. A mother partridge will pretend injury to decoy predators from her helpless nestlings and literally give her life for her children. The pear tree symbolizes the cross.
- Two turtle doves are the Old and New Testaments of the Bible.
- Three French hens: in the sixteenth century these birds were affordable only by the rich; they are signs for the three great gifts of faith, hope and love (1 Corinthians 13:13).
- Four calling birds are the four Gospels, Matthew, Mark, Luke and John.
- Five gold rings are the first five books of the Old Testament or the Torah. These books were treated by the Jews with reverence and were considered more valuable than gold (Psalm 19:10).
- Six geese a-laying. Eggs are a symbol of new life and the geese mark the six days of creation. God spoke the word and brought forth life.
- Seven swans a-swimming are the seven gifts of the Holy Spirit (Romans 12:6–8): prophecy, service, teaching, encouraging, giving, leadership and mercy.
- Eight maids-a-milking equal the eight Beatitudes of Jesus (Matthew 5:3–10), which nourish us as milk does.
- Nine ladies dancing represent the nine fruits of the Holy Spirit (Galatians 5:22–23): love, joy, peace, patience, kindness, goodness, faithfulness, gentleness and self-control.
- Ten lords a-leaping are the Ten Commandments (Exodus 20:3–17). Lords were men who carried social authority.
- Eleven pipers piping match the eleven apostles who stayed loyal to Jesus and the pipes express the people joyfully following their message.

- Twelve drummers drumming beat out the twelve vital beliefs that set us apart as Christians that are in the Creed of the Apostles.

It is tempting to go with this neat explanation. The numbers seem, as it were, to add up. However there are arguments against this idea, among them that this interpretation was a way for Christians to claim as one of their own what is actually a secular song. For example, all the items could just be birds: the calling birds might be a phonetic misunderstanding of 'colly' birds, a term used for blackbirds; gold rings are maybe 'goldspinks', the Scottish name for goldfinches, the mysterious pear tree could come from the French word for partridge, *perdrix*.

Who knows? Also, there are lots of variants of the gifts themselves in areas of Britain and beyond. In France for example, this carol is all about food, featuring wood pigeons, rabbits, ducks, hares, turkeys, hams, legs of mutton, partridges with cabbage, salads, and to complete the feast, twelve full casks of wine!

It is also possible that 'The Twelve Days of Christmas' was religious and inspired by number carols like 'The Seven Joys of Mary' or 'The New Dial', which takes the hours of the clock to relate Christian concepts. The folk song, 'Green Grow the Rushes-O', closely related to 'The New Dial', also has many concealed religious references. Whatever the truth of the matter, it's packed with glittering images.

I've performed this carol in *Songs of Praise* at the Royal Albert Hall as part of the Big Sing. It was a trio: Connie Fisher, who won BBC TV's *How Do You Solve a Problem Like Maria?* programme, and Ray Quinn of course, who was also on *The X Factor* (and came second to Leona Lewis). So to have these two reality TV performers and myself singing in the Albert Hall to a thousand people this particular piece was very strange. I remember Connie and Ray being very, very confident and saying that they knew the words and which part each was singing. And me of course in the middle. Going back to my chorister days I knew that first they hadn't sung it before publicly and then that they were the probationers.

Of course, what happened? Ray got his words wrong and Connie forgot that she was singing about four calling birds and instead sang about two turtle doves, so we could have got into a right mess. But the audience who were in the Hall that day for that recording loved the fact that we got it wrong. I think it added to the whole feeling of merriment that was already in the building. You can't but smile when you're performing carols.

The great thing about 'The Twelve Days of Christmas' is that even it you do mess it up you always know that you're going to get one line right and that's 'Five gold rings'. After that it's up to you, but that's the middle of the carol if you like, where all forces should come together in time. I have to be honest and say that I don't really take this carol that seriously. It's probably not one of my favourites, it's a bit of fun. It's very repetitive, and doesn't take you on a journey in any sense of the word. It hasn't got the majesty and triumphant aspect of some of the others, like 'Hark! The Herald Angels Sing' or 'O Come, All Ye Faithful'. It also lacks the mystery or the heart of something like 'O Come, O Come, Emmanuel' or 'Silent Night'. But it's a good little bit of Christmas froth.

FURTHER READING

Allen, William Francis; Ware, Charles Pickard; Garrison, Lucy McKim, *Slave Songs of the United States* (Oak Publications, New York, 1965)

Bradley, Ian C, *The Daily Telegraph Book of Carols* (Continuum, 2006)

Cairns, David, *Berlioz: Volume Two: Servitude and Greatness, 1832–1869* (University of California Press, 2000)

Dearmer, Percy; Vaughan Williams, R; Shaw, Martin, *The Oxford Book of Carols* (Oxford University Press, 1928, paperback 1964)

Jacques, Reginald and Willcocks, David, (eds), *Carols for Choirs 1* (Oxford University Press, 1961)

Keyte, Hugh and Parrott, Andrew (eds), *The New Oxford Book of Carols* (Oxford University Press, 1992)

Marsh, Jan, *Christina Rossetti: A Literary Biography* (Jonathan Cape, 1994)

Perry, Michael (ed.), *Carols for Today* (Hodder and Stoughton, 1986)

Reeves, Marjorie and Worsley, Jenyth, *Favourite Hymns: 2000 Years of Magnificat* (Continuum, 2001)

Roseberry, Eric (ed.), *The Faber Book of Carols and Christmas Songs* (Faber, 1983)

Routley, Erik, *The English Carol* (Oxford University Press, 1959)

Sandys, William, *Christmas Carols Ancient and Modern* (Richard Beckley, 1833)

Studwell, William, *The Christmas Carol Reader* (Harrington Park Press, 1995)

Vaughan Williams, Ursula, *R.V.W: A Biography of Ralph Vaughan Williams* (Oxford Lives, Oxford University Press, 1993)

Watson, J R, (ed.), *An Annotated Anthology of Hymns* (Oxford University Press, 2003)

ACKNOWLEDGEMENTS

Firstly, to my family, Claire, Emilia and Lucas for their love and support. I would be nothing without you. Love and thanks to Philippa Brewster for her never-ending positive nature and helping hand. To Georgina Capel and Anita Land for being them (scary at the best of times)! To Wendi Batt for being my right hand lady – cheers. To Trevor Dolby, Nicola Taplin and all at Preface and Random House – sorry for always being late and thanks for everything. To Peter Ward for the text design and Charlotte Abrams-Simpson for the jacket. To all at *Songs of Praise*, thanks for the great times. Thanks also to my publishers the Music Sales Group. To Adrian Sear and all at Demon Music Group who will be releasing a Carol CD to accompany this book. And a huge thanks to all the talented musicians and lyricists who came up with these festive treasures. Happy Christmas!